FROM THE EXTINCT VOLCANO, A BIRD OF PARADISE

Mongrel Empire Press
Norman, Oklahoma, United States of America

Norman, Oklahoma
2014

FIRST EDITION, 2014

From the Extinct Volcano, a Bird of Paradise
© 2014
by Carter Revard

ISBN 978-0-9851337-8-8

Except for fair use in reviews and/or scholarly considerations, no part of this book may be reproduced, performed, recorded, or otherwise transmitted without the written consent of the author and the permission of the publisher.

Cover Image
Singers at the Drum © 2014 Clarence Redcorn

Author Photo
Bob Bensen © 2009

MONGREL EMPIRE PRESS
NORMAN, OK

ONLINE CATALOGUE: WWW.MONGRELEMPIRE.ORG

This publisher is a proud member of

COUNCIL OF LITERARY MAGAZINES & PRESSES
www.clmp.org

Book design by Mongrel Empire Press using iWork Pages.

FROM THE EXTINCT VOLCANO, A BIRD OF PARADISE

Carter Revard

Edited and with a Foreword by Brian K. Hudson

Acknowledgments

"Doppelgängers: A Nativity Ode," "December Transients," and "Tumblebuggery" originally published in *Indigenous Bodies: Reviewing, Relocating, Reclaiming*, ed. Jacqueline Fear-Segal et al., SUNY Press, 2013.

"A Mandala of Sorts," "History Into Words," "Two Riddles: The Swan's Song, Pilotless Angel," and "Geode" originally published in *How The Songs Come Down*, Salt Publishers, Cambridge, England, 2005.

"Dancing with Dinosaurs" originally published in *Denver Quarterly*, 1980; reprinted in *Winning the Dust Bowl*, University of Arizona Press, 2001.

"Over By Fairfax, Leaving Tracks," "A Song That We Still Sing," and "Songs of the Wine-Throated Hummingbird" originally published in *Winning the Dust Bowl*, University of Arizona Press, 2001.

"Deer Mice Singing Up Parnassus" and "Æsculapius Unbound" originally published in *SING: Poetry from the Indigenous Americas*, ed. Allison Hedge Coke, University of Arizona Press, 2011.

"In Chigger Heaven" and "Given" originally published in *Cowboys and Indians, Christmas Shopping*, Point Riders Press, 1992.

"Dreaming in Oxford" originally published in *Yellow Medicine Review*, 2010.

"Driving in Oklahoma" originally published in *Ponca War Dancers*, Point Riders Press, 1980.

"Living In The Holy Land" and "Go to College" originally published in *Stand*, 2008.

"What The Eagle Fan Says," "November 1988 in Washington, D.C.," "Parading With The Veterans of Foreign Wars," "Outside in St. Louis," and "Earth and Diamonds" originally published in *An Eagle Nation*, University of Arizona Press, 1992.

"The Country's" originally published in *Denver Quarterly*, 1980.

"Prehistoric Surveillance in Bethlehem?" originally published in *Studies in American Indian Literatures*, 2014.

"Meadows, Moths, Slatebeds, Dictionaries" originally published in *Sentence*, 2009.

Contents

Foreword	i
A Note on Song, Speech, and Community-Making	iii
Doppelgängers: A Nativity Ode	1
A Mandala of Sorts	5
Dancing with Dinosaurs	6
December Transients	10
Deer Mice Singing Up Parnassus	11
Aesculapius Unbound	14
In Chigger Heaven	18
History Into Words	20
Dreaming in Oxford	21
Driving in Oklahoma	22
Coming Home from Columbus	23
Tumblebuggery: O Dea Moneta, Credit Our Belief	26
Living In The Holy Land	29
What the Eagle Fan Says	33
The Country's	35
Go to College	37
November 1988 in Washington D.C.	38
Parading with the Veterans of Foreign Wars	40
Outside in St. Louis	43
Given	45
Over by Fairfax, Leaving Tracks	47
Two Riddles: A Diptych	48
Earth and Diamonds	49
Geode	53
Transfigurations	55
A Song That We Still Sing	61
ESP Scan for 40th Birthday	63
The Prime Minister Explains	66
Prehistoric Surveillance in Bethlehem?	67
Libel Suit	71
The Body Politic	75
Meadows, Moths, Slatebeds, Dictionaries	78
Songs of the Wine-Throated Hummingbird	80
He Should of Drunk Goat's Milk Maybe	82
Terrace Haikus, Château de Lavigny	84

FOREWORD

In *From the Extinct Volcano, A Bird of Paradise*, Carter Revard focuses on song as a tool for cultural survival. His attention to cultural preservation insightfully includes songs by nonhuman beings. Revard sets this collection at an angle that can be usefully understood as Osage posthumanism. Posthumanist discourse shows concern with the possibility of knowledge outside anthropocentric, or human-centered, understanding. I do not use this phrase to reduce Osage ways of knowing to fit the latest trend in academic discourse. What I am suggesting is that posthumanism and Osage theories, along with many tribally-specific ways of understanding our place in the world, can flourish by being in conversation with one another. Revard belies anthropocentric formulations of humanity by placing his poems about Indigenous survival through song (such as "Living In The Holy Land" and "A Song We Still Sing") beside his poems about nonhuman animals (and other beings) who also survive through singing.

For those unfamiliar with Revard, I will sing briefly here of his life. He was born in 1931 in Pawhuska, Oklahoma. Revard grew up near Buck Creek, twenty miles from his birthplace, where he was raised by his mother and Osage stepfather. Through these family connections, he learned of his Osage and Ponca culture alongside the Irish and Scots-Irish influence of his mother. His formal education and that of his six siblings began in a one-room school. He trained greyhounds in his teen years. Revard attended Bartlesville College-High, where he won a radio quiz, which awarded him a scholarship to Tulsa University, where he earned a B.A. in English. He achieved a Rhodes scholarship in 1952, which led him to an M.A. at Oxford and a Ph.D. from Yale. It was at this time that Revard received his Osage name—Nompehwahthe (Fear-Inspiring)—by his grandmother, Mrs. Josephine Jump, in a traditional naming ceremony. His teaching career started at Amherst College, after which he quickly moved to Washington University in St. Louis, where Revard spent thirty-six years as a teacher and scholar. In addition to his teaching and scholarship in medieval literature, Revard has been an integral voice in the field of Native American literature since the early 1970s, publishing several collections of poetry. Revard has continued to be an active influence on the field, especially since his retirement in 1997. He is widely recognized as one of the most highly-respected Native poets. In 2005, Revard's contributions were acknowledged with the Lifetime Achievement Award from the Native Writers' Circle of the Americas.

As Revard remarks in his introductory note, *From the Extinct Volcano* sets some previously published poems alongside several new ones "to celebrate our creatural selves." In this collection, he demonstrates how song—as a foundational element of culture—is performed by human and nonhuman animals alike. In doing so, he shows us the hubris of anthropocentric assumptions that posit humans as the exceptional species in culture-making practices. Revard's attentiveness to the cultures of other animals is evident in the poems here. His close attention to the behavior of nonhuman animals (and the nonhuman world more generally) is reminiscent of the writings of another Osage author, John Joseph Mathews. Revard pays close attention to scientific accounts of animal behavior: drumming deer mice and the songs of several birds (including the wine-throated hummingbird), diligent dung beetles, egg-eating blacksnakes, and opportunistic chiggers—to name only a few of the species given attention in this collection. A personal favorite of mine is the reprinted "Dancing with Dinosaurs," in which Revard celebrates how the prehistoric creatures have "put on feathers and survived" in their evolutionary journey to become modern birds. He uses this poem to describe how Indigenous humans have done likewise, wearing feathers for ceremonies and surviving by adaptation. This poem redirects Indigenous Studies: instead of focusing on a static past, it transports readers into present and future forms of indigeneity.

But, again, it is not only human and nonhuman animals that sing in Revard's newest collection. Reminiscent of Osage philosopher George Tinker's argument for the possibility of understanding rocks as conscious beings, Revard broadens the scope of what it means to sing outside humanity. "Geode," for instance, is told from the point of view of the geological structure as it proceeds from early formation in the ocean to becoming bookends on a shelf. "Earth and Diamonds" ruminates on the process of diamond formation as a metaphor for scientific truths as narratives or how "we keep exploding facts / into old myths, and then compressing myths / into new facts." By illustrating the practices of song among human and nonhuman animals as well as those beings which we do not typically think of as living, Revard's newest collection of poetry shows readers an Osage epistemology that challenges the dominant anthropocentric narratives that have limited how we study culture.

Brian K. Hudson
University of Oklahoma

A Note on Song, Speech, and Community-Making

These poems are about migrations and mutations, how we and our fellow creatures move
through space and time and change but stay ourselves, individually and together—and about how singing helps us move and dancing helps us stay. I think it likely that creatures sang and danced before they spoke, and that communities were first made of song and dance: metron(o/y)mic mouth, hands, feet, bodies. Birds do it, bees do it, octopodes and people do it. And I suspect singing began from weeping and from laughing, turned into choral tragedy and comedy, kept time with rhythms and rhymes of tropical sunlight and starlight, temperate blossom and snowfall. Without song, no nesting. Home, as the Frost poem says, is where, when you go there, they have to take you in, and it turns out our relatives are everywhere. So the tropical paradise with snow around it in New Guinea, in the crater of a long-extinct volcano called Mount Bosavi, a place where new forms of life have evolved in isolation (including a Bird of Paradise, arising from that extinct volcano like a Phoenix), "rhymes" antipodally with the Osage Agency town where I was born, Pawhuska, which means "White Hair." Now song has put on feathers, we dance, sing, and speak with each other in Pawhuska, at the June solstice, to keep the Osage Nation alive. Our dances begin and end with spoken prayers. We hear Adam and Eve as Milton gives them to us, every dawn, if we are lucky enough to have birds as neighbors: "Never again," as the Frost sonnet tells us, "would birds' song be the same," so for them at sunrise, I believe, the Paradise within is happier far.

Not long after I wrote the paragraph above, I was happy to discover Iain McChristie's *The Master and his Emissary* (Yale University Press, 2009), whose third chapter, "Language, Truth, and Music" provides, as it seems to me, support for the paragraph's remarks about song and dance. (It goes well with Tim Birkhead's *The Wisdom of Birds*—Bloomsbury Press, 2008; and with Richard O. Prum's "Coevolutionary aesthetics in human and biotic artworlds," published online 06 July 2013 in *Biol Philos* with open access at *Springerlink.com*.)

Dr. McChristie, a psychiatrist who works with neuro-imaging, earned a D.Phil. in English literature at Oxford before turning to medicine and becoming a practicing psychiatrist and brain-researcher, and he therefore brings to his account of the bilateral brain and its evolutionary history in relation to music, speech, and human culture (and re-semblances to fellow creatures) a deep knowledge of literature and art, and a sensitive understanding of how poems work and what they may do for us.

Evolution of the human brain and social behavior is discussed also in *Social Brain, Distributed Mind*, edited by Robin Dunbar, Clive Gamble, and John Gowlett (Oxford University Press, 2010). As Lawrence Barham notes (p. 367), Dunbar's "social brain hypothesis" asserts that "the formation and maintenance of complex social relationships has been the driving selective force in primate cognitive evolution," and that "modern human behaviour is defined by the ability to form imaginative worlds, as exhibited in communal religion and storytelling . . . rooted in the social domain."

Clive Gamble, co-director of the British Academy Centenary Project "From Lucy to Language: The Archæology of the Social Brain," suggests (p. 34) that these were not the only way hominids could "extend social relations": "Social laughter and crying...heightens interaction through physiological benefits. This is also the case with singing and other forms of music-making accompanied by dance...." He suggests (Table 2.3, p. 33) that this level of social behavior (dance, music, crying, laughter) was reached perhaps a million years ago among small communities of *Homo habilis/ergaster*—at a time long after "Lucy" had left her footprints in the volcanic ash of Africa for Mary Leakey to discover in 1976 (for which, see Leakey's article in the 1982 *Scientific American* on those footprints at Laetoli). And of course we call her "Lucy" because when the Leakeys were digging fossils and footprints in Olduvai Gorge, the song being played over and over as they worked was "Lucy in the Sky with Diamonds...."

Long before Lucy, though, the little deer mice went singing up Parnassus with a choir of cicadas (the Muses' Daughters); Chaunteclere and Pertelote and the morning stars sang together; and all the Sons of God shouted for joy . . .

But (you say), if that's the case, if **SONG** matters so much, *why is it that poets can no longer sing for their suppers?*[1]   One possible answer would be: because the people CALLED poets (me, among others) no longer sing the news by which we live, communally and individually. That task has been given on the one hand to "rock stars," "rappers," "country singers,"[2] or "moviemakers"; and on the other hand to "scientists."

In this collection of poems, the news I am reporting/singing has in many instances been dug up by the "unacknowledged legislators of mankind" called "scientists," who I think are bringing us the gen-you-wine HISstory, HERstory, OURstory, THEIRstory of our time and the world we have been given. With them, I celebrate our creatural selves, I sing our polyphiloprogenitive selves, afloat on the Crossing Creation Ferry—whether one-way or round-trip, who can say?

If, for instance, we listened to what a solid-state physicist could tell us of "rare earths" and their uses in our time, or what a marine biologist could tell us about the living beings in tidal pools, we might hear some of the truest poems in our world at this time. And faint music from those poems does come through to quite a large audience—albeit they are not called "poems," but disguised as "popular science," in for example two "articles" printed in the June 2011 issue of *National Geographic*, within which there are poems waiting to put on rainbow wings: "Brimming Pools" by Mel White (pages 100-115), with marvelous photographs of creatures from tidal pools by David Littschwager; and "The Secret Ingredients of (almost) Everything," by Tim Folger (pages 136-45), about "rare earths" and their uses in smart phones and laptops, MRI scans, hybrid cars, wind turbines, tinted sunglasses and wine-bottle glass, Predator drones and Tomahawk cruise missiles. Or, sometimes, poems might be disguised as "TV documentaries," on hummingbirds say, or on Mount Bosavi and its snow-surrounded tropical paradise. Archæologists, geologists, astrophysicists, "pure mathematicians," neurolinguists, nanotechnologists, all those nerds dowsing with smart-phones for wormhole-springs bubbling up from future worlds—they don't have eyes as good as those of Chaunteclere, or ears as good as those of little grey bats or rock-doves, but where they lead me I will surely try to follow.

Yet crossing into eternity, whatever the fee may be, I want to bring along the past: in what once was called "junk" DNA there are pearls of great price, as also in our Osage Creation Stories. We make, and learn, new songs, but we sing the old ones too. Deer mice, humpback whales, orchard orioles: a skylark's songs may be—as Shelley, using Milton's word, said—*unpremeditated*, but psalms may be meme-orized.

Carter Revard
Indian Country

---

[1] My reference here is to English-speaking countries. The evidence is very different in, for instance, Arabic-speaking countries, as witness the vital role of songs and singers in (for instance) Tahrir Square in Cairo during the 2011 demonstrations that overthrew the Mubarak regime.

[2] Michael Chabon, in "Let It Rock" (*New York Review of Books* LX, No. 12, July 11, 2013), says (p. 27) that over the past thirty years he has written "poems so disputable that no one apart from me has ever considered them to be poems at all...everyone who looks at them seems to regard them as novels...but to me they have always felt like poems...." He considers then the impact of song lyrics on his own writing. On the one hand, he says, (p. 28), "rock lyrics could not really be poetry because when you took away the melody, the instrumentation, and above all the voice of the singer, a song lyric just kind of huddled there on a page looking plucked and forlorn, like Foghorn Leghorn after a brush with the Tasmanian Devil....I had always felt a sense of exaltation at the end of that song when I listened to *Sgt. Pepper*, as ascending angelic voices triumphantly asserted 'She . . . is having...FUN...' But typed out on a ditto, those words had looked banal, trivial . . . " Yet, Chabon insists, "Dylan's lyrics are *writing*, and as writing they have influenced my own writing. In fact, song lyrics in general have arguably mattered to and shaped me more, as a writer, than novels or short stories written by any but the most crucial of my literary heroes....the words...of rock, soul, and hip-hop constitute the body of writing that I know best...[they] are the only written works that I have ever reliably committed to memory, apart from a touch of Poe, a smidgen of Kipling's 'If,' bits and pieces of Shakespeare." Thinking it over, he wonders whether "...the stories that fiction writers tell, their characters and settings, are only the lyrics to a song the writer is called upon to sing and play," and he says finally, "But the stories and characters won't come alive . . . until you . . . throw back your head, open your mouth, and let it rock."

I gratefully acknowledge here a June 2011 residency at the Château de Lavigny in Switzerland that helped me rethink all these poems, rewrite some of them, and write some new ones.
~Carter Revard

DOPPELGÄNGERS: A NATIVITY ODE
If only Columbus had . . .

By way of introduction: It has lately been discovered that, just as the first stanza of this piece narrates, at a certain time of year hellacious gales of wind blow from east to west through certain parts of the Sahara (the "Bodélé Depression"), from which they scoop great quantities of very fine minerals, sweeping them up into dark roiling clouds that are then driven high across the Atlantic, over Brazil and up along the Amazon and its tributaries, where the fine dust eventually settles down into the lush rainforests. (For scientific accounts of this, see *Deflation in the dustiest place on Earth: The Bodélé Depression, Chad*, in *Geomorphology*, Volume 105, Issues 1-2, 1 April 2009, Pages 50-58; and *Proceedings of the National Academy of Sciences of the United States of America*, December 8, 2009, vol. 106 no. 49, 20564-20571.) It is thought that this Sahara dust constitutes exactly the fertilizing soils and minerals required to renew those rain forests, which otherwise would deplete the soils so extensively that eventually the forests would die. In this way, desert and jungle are "Doppelgängers," the orchid ("air-plant," epiphyte) an apotheosis of hurricane (Hart Crane's wonderful poem "The Air Plant" reversed), nectar an avatar of dust. If we had the ability of angels to see past and present and future simultaneously, we might see jungles that used to cover what is now the Sahara, and perhaps a desert that will cover what are now the rain forests of Brazil; but for now, I have painted only two brothers, African desert and Brazilian rainforest, in present time. Not dust to dust, but dust into nectar, is the story of Terra Nuova.

    For my poem, I have put that story together with another of an infant's finding his voice, first in weeping and then in laughing, which are also Doppelgängers, and have narrated this in terms of the Osage Creation Story's account of our people's having come down into this world from the stars. So the Infanta Nuova, made of stardust (though not named Ziggy), asleep in a dark house, awakes in pre-dawn darkness and cries, is cleansed, sung to, sings along with the strong-heart song, and is fed, then sees through the window the Morning Star and the Dawn, and hears a bird sing, at which (s)he laughs, and sings along with it the new/old song of joy, one of our Osage songs.

    In my first year on Earth, my twin sister and I were taken care of for some time by our Ponca aunt Jewell MacDonald in the village at White Eagle, Oklahoma. A lullaby she used to sing us, made by her blind great aunt, is the Strong Heart Song she sings in the poem, made to hearten the warriors in despair, driven from their homelands in the Dakotas down to White Eagle in Oklahoma. The old voice is Aunt Jewell's mother, who—waked again at dawn by the child's voice—rises and (like a Ponca Firebird) fixes sun-golden pancakes with honey and fresh butter for breakfast—something gold that sticks to the ribs, a contrafactum to the Frost lyric "Nothing Gold Can Stay." (Contrafacta are two or more lyrics sung to the same tune—in medieval times, these might involve turning a pastourelle about a young girl's wooing into a lament spoken by Mary at the Cross; or, in the case of the "Cuckoo Song"—"Sumer is icumen in"—an Easter hymn. In my poem, I have reversed Frost's exquisite brief lyric, in which his line "So dawn goes down to day" implies a falling-off in beauty; my contrafactual version is that the ongoing life in the house, now filled with daylight, is a feasting and not a falling off.) And I have stuffed into the final line both *Lycidas (in italics)* and the Lord's Prayer.

1.

It's not exactly a Pentecostal wind, hardly
the Niña, Pinta, and Santa Maria, more
a haboob or maybe simoom, it's just
a burning desert blast at this time of the year—
down on the southern Sahara swoops a hellish
roiling hurricane-force wind that scoops
a hundred-mile-long rift-full of dusty crystals up
and up and drives them in dark flashing clouds westward
high and higher and out over the coastline of Africa, the grey
haze now streaming across the Atlantic over Brazil
and on up over the Amazon,
high above lush rain-forests until the fine
dust comes delicately down into an orchid's apotheosis
of hurricane where a hummingbird
glittering sends its long tongue into
deep nectar, avatar
of Sahara sand.

2.

—In this dark house I hear the
shimmering of my Doppelgänger's wings,
but I am crying, the voices say—
some time ago I came down like dust
from the stars into this house where the *old voice* says
he is crying, give him
some milk, it says,
and the *young voice* says
*I have to **change** him first,*
then hands come down and take me up,
remove the swaddling clothes and dip
me in chilly water, wash me clean,

and I am crying and the *young voice* sings,
I still myself and listen, I hear the words,
"*What are you afraid of?*" they say,
"*No one can go around death.*"
In this dark house there are no
stars but there is song, the hands
have warmed a bottle, there is milk,
but first I sing along, the *young voice* stops then
and I sing alone,
"*What are we afraid of, no one
can go around death.*"
My brother hears me and he turns
from the nectar and flies out
into the moonlight, and the stars
are over him. "*This child
is singing,*" the young voice says, and then
the old voice says,
"*Give him the bottle, let him sleep.*"
The milk is sweet and warm. Now
through silent window
the morning star comes nearer,
then fades away, the east turns russet and my brother
the orchard oriole, wearing the soft
colors of early dawn, begins to sing,
so I laugh and sing,
we sing together
without words his song of joy,
"*The stars go home and now
the sun appears,*"
then the old voice says,
"*I guess I better get up
and fix some breakfast now*"—
so dawn goes down to day,
its light-gold pancakes lifting off a tray
like little suns, butter and honey melting,
black coffee's bitter perfume rising while
Grandmother gives us, **yet once more**, our daily lives.

Notes to **Doppelgängers: A Nativity Ode**

When I was a boy in the Buck Creek Valley on the Reservation, one spring and summer a pair of orchard orioles nested in the elms beside our home, and I learned to whistle their challenge-notes and the long cascading series of mellifluous notes of their song. Alexander F. Skutch (*Orioles, Blackbirds, and their Kin*, University of Arizona Press, 1996), studied them in their winter migration homes in Central America and says the orchard orioles were "most songful of all the birds I have heard . . . At dawn, young and old sang together in a many-voiced chorus of whistled notes delightful to hear" (p. 190). He reported also that sometimes, while the female was in the nest, she sang a response to her mate's song.

A Mandala of Sorts
The jewel is in the lotus: *a mantra*

This windless October eve the dusk comes down
As through endless depths, and settles slowly,
Recoiling on itself, among dark branches
Of elm trees where rain gleams like iron
Around robins hopping nervous as minnows,
Setting out, this night, through the mist and rain.

Out by the street-crossing a lamp flares on and
Loosens white house-walls from the swaying darkness
Like lotus-petals for the lamp's electric jewel,
White corner houses, black-backed, where neighbors
Sleep in the dazzled night, locked in whiteness,
Sleep and live, within their jeweled lotus.

I don't know how they live. Here at the edge
Of lamplight I can hear the low cries of birds leaving
And southward flying, down the edge of day,
That bloodred circle where the spinning earth
Is stained with sunset while the rose of dawn
Petals its dust with momentary bloom—

And I watch go riding down the gutter a feather
Spinning and twinkling, left by one of those birds
Whirled behind summer down the earth's tilting
Into the dawn, or across dark seas to shores
Hushed by their singing, where sunburned lovers lie
Among stars at dusk, and watch the gold moon rise.

DANCING WITH DINOSAURS

I was delighted when archaeologists noticed that dinosaurs have not died out, that what we hear singing at the windowsill is a tiny tyrannosaurus, as the earthworms have always known, trembling at the thunderous tread of a robin bobbing across the lawn to gobble them down. I had loved to hear the birds begin their prayers, of a summer's morning in the Buck Creek valley, as naturally as Milton's Adam and Eve sang matin-psalms in Eden. I always was mystified by their migrations, and I wondered what they had in mind as they darted up into the air of Louisiana and set sail for Yucatan. What maps do they use, what ancestral voices do they hear prophesying spring where they are headed?

Then I read in *National Geographic* and *Scientific American* of how the tiny black-and-white warblers in Nova Scotia and Maine take off in September and fly for three days and nights, Good Friday to Easter Sunday as it were, at the cold height of twenty thousand feet or more, over the whole Atlantic Ocean down to South America. I was not surprised, but I was and am amazed.

So when news came that even archaeologists now admitted what any careful observer of a back yard had always known, that these were small dinosaurs who had put on feathers and survived, I suddenly understood better why we as Indian people put on our feathers to survive. I wished once again that the anthropologists who keep digging in the earth for our bones would listen for our songs in the air. We are extinct as dinosaurs, we are alive as birds. So I put into the poem's first half the story of dinosaurs turning into birds, back when the Atlantic Ocean was just flowing into existence between the great separating pieces of Pan-Gæa (the monster continent/pregnant). I imagined the small birds learning to fly and sing, and launching out over this new Atlantic Ocean from what would become Nova Scotia, and winging high over Bermuda, all the way down to perch on Venezuela, the left shoulder of South America, performing what I had lately learned of the small black-and-white warblers, who had recently been tracked with radar as they performed that three-day non-stop flight, their Trail of Songs, that passage of three days and nights, through darkness and light from death to life, that brave journey of small beings weighing only a few ounces, flying from winter into spring. And I ended the poem's first half with praise of those birds whose feathers we carry in our ceremonies, *who made their rainbow bodies long before we came to earth, who learning song and flight became beings for whom the infinite sky and trackless ocean are a path to spring.*

And because I was just then learning to be a Gourd Dancer, I wrote in the poem's second half of our dancing in St. Louis when we brought into the circle of named beings the Comanche granddaughter of Bob and Evelyne Wahkinney Voelker, and how, as the gourds shook and their feathers fluttered, we knew that now she could cross with us. Here now, on the following pages, is the poem for all our relations:

1.
Before we came to earth,
before the birds had come,
they were dinosaurs, their feathers
were a bright idea
that came this way:
see, two tiny creatures weighing
two ounces each keep quiet and among
the ferns observe bright-eyed
the monsters tear each other
and disappear; these two watch from
the edge of what, some fifty billion spins
of the cooling earth ahead, will be
called Nova Scotia—now, with reptilian
whistles they look southward as
Pan-Gaea breaks apart and lets
a young Atlantic send its thunder crashing
up to the pines where they cling
with minuscule bodies in a tossing wind,
September night in the chilly rain and
they sing, they spread
small wings to flutter out above
surf-spray and rise to
twenty thousand feet on swirling
winds of a passing cold front that lift
them over the grin of sharks southeastward into sun
and all day winging under him pass high above
the pink and snowy beaches of Bermuda flying
through zero cold and brilliance into darkness
then into moonlight over steel
Leviathans with their mimic pines that call them down
to rest and die—
they bear
southeast steadily but the Trade Winds come and
float them curving
back southward over the Windward Islands and
southwestward into marine and scarlet of
their third day coming down
to four thousand feet, still winging over
Tobago, descending till
the scaly waves stretch and feather into the surf of
Venezuela,
and they drop

through moonlight down to
perch
on South America's shoulder, having become
the Male and Female Singers, having
put on their feathers and survived.

2.
When I was named
a Thunder person, I was told:
here is a being
of whom you may make your body
that you may live to see old age: now
as we face the drum
and dance shaking the gourds, this gourd
is like a rainbow of feathers, lightly
fastened with buckskin,
fluttering as the gourd is shaken.
The eagle feathers I
have still not earned, it is
the small birds only
whose life continues on the gourd,
whose life continues in our dance,
that flutter as the gourd is rattled and
we dance to honor on a sunbright day
and in the moonbright night
the little girl being brought in,
becoming one of us,
as once was done for me,
for each of us who dance.
The small birds only, who have given
their bodies that a small girl
may live to see old age.
I have called them here
to set them into song
who made their rainbow bodies long before
we came to earth,
who learning song and flight became
beings for whom the infinite sky
and trackless ocean are
a path to spring:
now they will sing and we
are dancing with them, here.

December Transients

First snow four inches deep, a half
moon white gold as twilight darkens and Blanca—
off-leash, racing in circles, panting with joy—hurls herself
down and rolls, and snuffs, and wriggles into new
half-fluff, half-sleet gleaming beneath
dark trunks and leafless branches in
the little park, leaps up and grins
trotting back to Lawrence, who cocks his head
and looks up saying, "Geese!"
as the creaking honks come faintly down
from darkness, and overhead appear, spot-lit *in*
the golden lightning of the sunken sun
and soaring moon, a ragged V of geese out of darkness
floating, shifting and milling overhead,
uncertain whether to pause, and then
they reform as three move to the lead, the lines
tighten and they head southwestward into
the afterglow and are gone.
Who ever could
have thought, watching the small
dinosaurs shiver while the first
brilliant snowflakes came down into
their world so newly cold, that a small
black Border Collie would take such joy
in running through that snow
with featherless biped friends, while dinosaur cousins
with feathers, calling to the moon and sun, would soar
above them brilliant as snowflakes, on their way
into that world of living waters toward which,
this night, they fly away.

Note: The italicized words are two lines stolen from Shelley's *To A Skylark*.

DEER MICE SINGING UP PARNASSUS[3]
for Bill and Lois Winchester

Sally Carrighar, in a meadow one night, heard what seemed a bird trilling, then saw it was a deer mouse. My friend Bill Winchester tells me that when deer mice came into his house from the tallgrass prairie of Oklahoma, he live-trapped and released them in a nearby hedgerow, but they waltzed back in, singing an epithalamium. Latin Musa, Greek Mousa, English Muse/Mouse linked by O—license to party on Parnassus and drink from Helicon. Reepicheep, Sir Toby, Sir Andrew & Feste (grilling Malvolio about Pythagorean metempsychoses), can join them in a catch, a coranto, a galliard, jig, or sink-a-pace, singing to Moon and Stars, Diana and Venus. Blake's Sunflower seeks that sweet golden clime where the Traveler's journey is done—but the little Deer Mice got there before tourists with FOX2P genes arrived: see NY Times 29 May 2009, p.A5, which reports that human "language gene" put into mice deepens their baby-cries, so we may before long have Mezzo Mice in our meadows.

      In this "new" world they sing,
                            as we come down from the stars,[2]
   like Milton's Leonora singing
             (aut Deus, aut vacui certé mens tertia cœli),[3]
       they climb up the stems
     of sunflowers still not weary
                    of time, and they trill,
      perching and swinging in
    meadow and glade as if
              a rainbow
     trout might rise
                to May-flies from their
   music, as if John Muir and
           Hetch Hetchy[4]
                   might come back
  alive and listening,
            anadromous as salmon or sabretooth
 tigers, up time itself into the glistening
                moonlit sonatas of
                        Sierra song.

Notes to **Dear Mice Singing Up Parnassus**

¹ From the November 23, 1974 *Nature Bulletin No. 545-A: Of the Forest Preserve District of Cook County, Illinois,* a description of *Deer Mice and White-Footed Mice*

At night, sitting on a wooded shore, waiting for fish to bite or quietly gazing into the coals of a camp fire, you often become aware of mysterious small noises nearby in the darkness . . . *you may hear a tiny drumming sound or a musical buzzing hum* . . . you have disturbed the night life of a wild mouse. *He makes the drumming sound by rapidly tapping a dry leaf or hollow stem with his front feet. Unlike house mice, his voice is more of a song than a mere squeak* . . . The *deer mouse* is an inhabitant of prairies, weedy fields, fencerows and roadsides. Its nests are often found under rocks, boards, haystacks and corn shocks. . . . In contrast, the *white-footed mouse* is a dweller of forests, brushlands and wooded river bottoms. It is a good climber and uses its long tail to balance it when running along twigs in search of food. Its nest may be in a fallen log or under a stump but, more often, it is in a woodpecker hole, a bird house, or an abandoned bird nest over which it builds a roof. They seldom come into our houses but often invade empty summer cottages where they make themselves snug homes in chair cushions, mattresses and stored clothing . . . They do not hibernate. After every fresh snow their tiny tracks show where they have been foraging the night before.

² In our Osage naming ceremonies it is said that we have come to this world from the stars. The words in one of our dawn-songs say of the Sun: "He returns, he is coming again into the visible world."

³ For Milton's epigram *Ad Leonoram Romæ cantentem*, of which this is line 5, see JOHN MILTON, Complete Shorter Poems, ed. Stella Revard (Wiley-Blackwell, 2009), p. 199, where a note explains: "This and the two epigrams following were composed either in late 1638 or early 1639 for the famous Neapolitan singer Leonora Baroni, whom Milton heard sing during one of his visits to Rome. She was later celebrated by Italian poets in a volume of commemorative poetry, *Applausi Poetici alle Glorie della Signora Leonora Baroni* (Rome, 1639)." The English verse translation (by Lawrence Revard, on p. 199) is:

> A winged angel from heaven's ranks itself is made
>   guard to each of us. Believe this, people.
> What wonder, Leonora, if your glory's greater,
>   for your voice itself sounds God's presence.

> Surely God or an emptied heaven's third intelligence,
> > hidden, empowering, glides through your throat,
> empowering, glides and simply teaches mortal hearts
> > to grow accustomed to immortal sound.
> For if God's all, and fused with all, then within you
> > he speaks as one and, silent, holds the rest.

For *mens tertia* "third intelligence," the editor cites Ficino's *Commentary* on Plato's *Symposium* 2.4.

[4] John Muir tried to save a Sierra vale, Hetch Hetchy, but the dam was built and now the people of San Francisco (St. Francis?) drink, shower, and flush with water drawn from that sanctuary—the moving waters at their priestlike task, as Keats says.

Il Piccolo Pavarotti
(*Peromyscus californicus*)

AESCULAPIUS UNBOUND
Ovid and Darwin in Oklahoma[1]

By beautiful design, a snake's jawbones
unhinge, so it can swallow
things bigger around
than it is.
I wondered, when
the old man shot a blacksnake in
the hen-house, then held it
up by the tail,

just how in hell those great big lumps
along its six-foot length, slow-twisting up and
down as it hung, had ever been
choked down.

Later, I heard that snakes
are deaf, those three hinged bones
had not yet turned into the malleus, incus
and stapes of my middle ear,
they have no tympanum
and no cochlea,

no auditory nerve, their brain only
processes earth's vibrations, but not thunder's,
so snakes don't sing, although perhaps
they dance when mating—
only their cousins, the small birds,[2]
sing the light's changes,
as Melampous knew.[3]

> So when I heard,
> as twilight grew, the orchard
> oriole sing its heart out there in the elm's
> Edenic shadows, something unhinged
> and let the music in,
>
> but if they hold me up and listen,
> it may by then be part of me—
> be how I live and breathe,
> or will at least be how
> I try to whistle, when
> the spirit moves.[4]

Notes to **Aesculapius Unbound**

¹In Ovid's *Metamorphoses*, Book 15 (lines 622-744), he tells how Apollo's son Æsculapius, god of healing, changed himself into the great serpent which twines about his staff, and as a serpent was brought by the Romans from the ancient Greek shrine in Epidaurus to Rome and installed, as the God of Healing, in a new shrine on an island in the Tiber, where he healed the Romans of a terrible plague. Earlier in Book 15, Ovid's spokesmen tell how the world was created and continually changes (humans are reincarnated, and some in previous lives were animals); they advocate a vegetarian diet instead of killing and eating sheep, goats, and oxen, and deplore animal sacrifices to the gods. Finally, Ovid ends this last book of his *Metamorphoses* by narrating recent and future Roman history: Julius Caesar's assassination and his transformation into a god (a star in heaven); the ascent to imperial power of Caesar's adopted son Augustus Caesar; and the future ascent to heaven of Augustus, who will "there, removed from our presence, listen to our prayers." In the last nine lines of the poem, Ovid prophesies that his poetry will also be immortal: "through all the ages shall I live in fame."

² This at least is the Darwinian Creation Story, as told in encyclopedias under the entry for *Reptiles*. This story says birds and snakes evolved as branches of *Reptilia*, and that mammals bloomed on another branch of that tree, so we humans (including the Oklahoma cowboy who shot the egg-stealing snakes, and the boy who witnessed that and heard an orchard oriole sing) also hang, not far away, on this tree of life.

³ See George Economou, *Ananios of Kleitor* (Exeter, England: Shearsman Books, 2009), Fragment 18, "Melampous overheard the worms overhead" (p. 20) and the *Endnote* on this, pp. 88-9, for the story of Melampous, who received the gift of hearing and understanding the speech of animals, and consequently the gift of prophecy, from some serpents, because he had ceremonially cremated the body of their mother whom he had found, "a sacrificial victim, beside an oak tree. In gratitude…these serpent children licked his ears as he slept, purifying him and enabling him to understand the language of birds and animals, which he used to foretell the future." Thanks, George: sometimes the gifts borne by Greeks are better than Trojans.

⁴*Acts of the Apostles* 2.1-6:

> 1. And when the day of Pentecost was fully come, they were all with one accord in one place.

2. And suddenly there came a sound from heaven as of a rushing mighty wind, and it filled all the house where they were sitting.

3. And there appeared to them cloven tongues like as of fire, and it sat upon each of them.

4. And they were all filled with the Holy Ghost and began to speak with other tongues, as the Spirit gave them utterance.
[. . .]
6. . . . every man heard them speak in his own language.

IN CHIGGER HEAVEN

We grew up crossing
the bluestem meadow full of flowers
in May, when butterflies were coming out to meet
the flowers at last as equals, like
equations that have found
their Ein(Philosopher's)Stein and can sip the nectar
of hyperspace at will,
and when also
were hatching out the tiny scarlet
chiggers, holding up their hooks
for rides toward heaven,
not on brilliant wings but into
the skin and making keratin cocktails
of huge paradisal monsters like us.
Well, *noblesse oblige*—
like angels, we
took them into eternity as far
that day as they were going, helping them
believe in Providence. Maybe
to angels,
when they come down to snuff
wild flowers of gratitude or skunks
of treachery, time is only
a chigger-bite they carry back to heaven,
or maybe souls
can't change until they've tapped into
red lasers pulsing under
the bright skin of stars. Maybe
every infinitesimal
eleven-dimensioned string
wiggles into a downy
angelic wing and flies to places
it does not see,
like scarlet chiggers on a redwinged
blackbird's epaulette, or like
the blackbird's feet not grasping,
within the wire it's on,

the good news from Jerusalem or
a quasar at this universe's edge. To lie down
in green pastures and get up
as Providence—
that is, with chiggers—
may not be a sign
of misspent youth, but I wonder who
is itching with these words,
within what space and time.

HISTORY INTO WORDS

In 1645-6, while besieged in Oxford by Cromwellian forces, King Charles I used Christ Church, with its Cathedral, as headquarters. A century before, King Henry VIII, by creating the new Diocese of Oxford, had transformed this former Parish Church of St. Frideswide into a Cathedral.

        I think of John Roberts, historian and
              Warden of Merton College, writing
    a History Of Europe, walking
           in late September maybe,
down the broad
        caramel-gravelled walk between
Christ Church Cathedral and Merton Meadows. The sky
    is blue this afternoon with high
cloud-puffs so bright they make
        him squint glancing up. When he looks through
the locked and steel-barred gate,
           past the wall's grey stones,
  past flowers at its base and edging
        the gate's both sides, he looks
  over a shaven lawn and at the smallest
cathedral in England. Crimson and creamy
          gate-roses frame the spire, a blue
sky edges its shadowed walls. Then between
        the gate's black bars a breath
of breeze brings scintillation and his eyes
       now focus on a billowing web,
  its small and gently flexing circles holding
  this butterfly of time whose wings mother
    our hurricanes, this delicate
      fossil jihad,
  this small cathedral, in its silken orb.

DREAMING IN OXFORD

Four a.m. in Oxford, I waked remembering
part of the dream—sitting
with Robert Frost and an unknown woman
I vaguely knew—she was
white-haired, looked like Grace Paley, who
had just died, or maybe
the Muse—
she had us playing this game,
to sit and notice how mistakes allow
truth to appear—yes, she said,
you're hiding in your hands
behind you, Robert, the Vanishing Red, and
he laughed and said, but look
sideways down this book-filled shelf,
see how it leads directly to a river
with luminous swans. Mister Frost,
I said, yesterday we walked that way,
Stella and I, past Lewis Carroll's rooms
along a graveled path
between the huge and whispering poplars and
the chattering tourists, down
to the Isis, and a swan came over
unhurriedly and took from looking-glass water pieces
of bread-crust that we threw to him and to
a powerboat coot and diffident moor-hen.
Yes, bakers
don't know who eats their bread,
you don't look straight at
a star, but just beside it, I said, the truest poetry
is the most feigning, this Osage reads your poems
over and over, they make my life
go better, and he laughed. It was still dark
when I waked up, but the dream
took me downstairs to let me see from a side
window the sun as it quietly
comes up and—
for another day at least—
the light is here.

DRIVING IN OKLAHOMA

On humming rubber along this white concrete,
lighthearted between the gravities
of source and destination like a man
halfway to the moon
in this bubble of tuneless whistling
at seventy miles an hour from the windvents,
over prairie swells rising
and falling, over the quick offramp
that drops to its underpass and the truck
thundering beneath as I cross
with the country music twanging out my windows,
I'm grooving down this highway feeling
technology is freedom's other name when
                                        —a meadowlark
comes sailing across my windshield
with breast shining yellow
and five notes pierce
the windroar like a flash
of nectar on mind,
gone as the country music swells up and drops
me wheeling down
my notch of cement-bottomed sky
between home and away
                                and wanting
to move again through country that a bird
has defined wholly with song,
and maybe next time see how
he flies so easy, when he sings.

Coming Home from Columbus

THEY'LL want to know, the great
grandchildren, how their ancestors
survived the hardships of our primitive
travels in the Age of Gasoline. So,
at 2:49 pm Central time here I am
Feste-nating in a Focus—not quite bombing along
but bombinating[1] at least—or maybe madly Malvoliating
through Illinois, with hey ho the wind, the wind,
and my God the rain—almost shoving me off-road, beating
from north-northwest on windows, surfing dark rain
and mist over me and these ginormous
double-semis snaking alongside
shaking and ready to topple, some right
behind tailgating up my exhaust, others
blocking both lanes in front, fending off
both me and the big bus-assed SUVs that keep
looming up, horning in and fishtailing as
they slip into blinding eddies off the trucks, then
muscling into the fizz ahead or at
the side or close behind—the thing
to do is not slow down, just watch
for the brilliant red in front that might
mean crash or spinout or steady as
she goes, prayers doubtless thicker than
the brown leaves flying at us in the blast
from thickets on the north side of this
east-west Interstate—and then,
briefly becalmed, between
the files of low fast clouds and rain that fly
into us every few miles—coming out
round a curve on a high overpass there's a hanging
seagull sixty feet above me, just under
the cloud-rack's ragged bottom, trying
to fly across the road, flapping desperately but
barely staying in place until at last it
gives up and is carried

backward to darkness on extended wings
—lucky this isn't
snow and ice, or we'd be doing
Extreme Snowboarding off some overpass,
but the road in front
brightens, the wind dies down, the rain
lets up, I pull into
a filling station and there
I let Big George get me a hot
chocolate with extra cream, I fill
the gas tank of my faithful little
four-cylinder "Bubbly," empty my bladder, then leave
the truckers to Circe and Demodocus
with Golden Oldies on his I-Pod,
and once more hit the Asphalt Trail
westward to Eden, or at least
Saint Louis.

And by God, the little champagne-gold
Focus moves our Selves four hundred miles
in seven hours, almost a cannonball run,
and we're welcomed home by
La Stella Mia when we roll
into St. Louis from Columbus, and we Tele-
phone son Stephen in Columbus, so
he'll not be worrying—

and that, Grandchildren,
is how we manage to survive
hard traveling, in the early Twenty-First
Century, here in the Classical Mid-West.

Notes to **Coming Home from Columbus**

[1] The entry for *Bombinate* in the Shorter OED defines it as "to buzz," dating first use as 1880, and supplying as sole illustrative quotation, in brackets, this: [RABELAIS, II. vii, *Questio subtilissima, utrum chimera in vacuo bombinans posit comedere secundas intentiones.*] This seemed to me appropriate for a Mini-Odyssey. My learned friend George Economou, however, points out that the Rabelais "quote," as found in his Everyman edition, is the title of one of many works listed in the catalogue of books found in II.vii.. The full title reads*:* "*Quaestio subtilissima, utrum Chimaera in vacuo bombinans possit comedere secundas intentiones, et fuit debatuta per decem hebdomadas in Consilio Constantiensi."* M. Economou adds that *bombinans*, as one would expect of Rabelaisian parody, here carries a scatological meaning, and translates the passage thus: "The most subtle question, whether the Chimera, farting away in a void, can eat its second intentions, was debated for ten weeks at the Council of Constance." As for what the "second intentions" might be, or how related to bombinating, I leave that to the learned Council members. My Self Mover and I, with no time for second intentions, might say with Hamlet, "[We] eat the air, promise-crammed."

TUMBLEBUGGERY: O DEA MONETA, CREDIT OUR BELIEF
Oklahoma and Wall Street, 2008

In-CRED-ible, what those brilliant
tumblebugs would do, out in our deep
bluestem meadow there on the Osage
Reservation, where placid cows in August daily and nightly
deposited their sloppy green
hendiadys, treasure and feast. Who knew,
when we would step with care,
barefoot as we were, around
those piles of green cowshit as we walked, on our way
to bring the cows back home and milk them,
how those dark-suited Scarab Beetles
assumed the role of global bankers, working
to "speed the process of converting
manure to substances usable
by other organisms"?[1] As barefoot kids, of course,
in Dust Bowl Oklahoma, we knew bankers
not at all, nor had we yet looked closely at
the back side of George Washington (on such green
money as poor kids had, a dollar bill),
where it looked back at us, that shining eye
of all-foreseeing Providence
inside the Great Seal of the United States, atop
its Pyramid, encircled by that pious, that august,
that Empire-founding invocation borrowed from
Ascanius, son of Æneas,
Annuit Coeptis Novus Ordo Seclorum.[2]
And even when we kids knelt and watched a shiny
tumblebug rolling, rolling, turning upside
down and pushing with her hind feet onward
the lucreous globe of shit she'd made,
and we saw her pause,
and scurry round to where
she'd dug the hole just big enough, measuring with
antennæ twiddling,
then shove and shove the ball down and in,
and go in after—I think we didn't know
that she'd be laying eggs just where

each hatchling's mouth would find a feast,
before she came back out, retraced her trail and started
to shape another global deal almost
worthy of Ares, money-changer of dead bodies,
or Melville's Confidence Man.[3]
We laughed at her solemn scurrying, all
klutzy but precise—although the more we looked,
the more we saw how purposeful she was.[4] Yet even if
our one-room school had owned
an old encyclopedia, we'd surely not have
looked under "dung beetle"
to see what we were seeing: that wasn't
what we called them, let alone
"Scarab Beetles"—so none of us, scrabbling there
in our August Dust Bowl, would have looked through a
Britannica, or an Insect Bible, back into
that old Egyptian Empire where embalmers placed
on Amenhotep's breast a Sacred Scarab, the
Tumblebug of Immortality that signified
the Sun rolling the dark ball of Earth and with
"the 30 segments of its six legs [standing for]
the 30 days of each month,"[5]
but even if we had, I think some smart twice-born kid
(Dionysian, Christian, or In-di-genous?)
might just have said: no wonder Pharaoh gave
Columbus so little credit that he left
the Pyramids behind and shook the dust
of Egypt from his feet and emigrated from
that ancient Dust Bowl to our green
and Promissory Land of Con-fidential
and Pyramidal Credit,
America.

Notes to **Tumblebuggery**

[1] *Encyclopædia Britannica: Micropædia III (Chicago, 1983), s.v. dung beetle*, p. 709.

[2] *Wikipedia* says the Great Seal was created in 1782 by commission from the Continental Congress, explaining the motto thus: *The Eye over it [the pyramid] and the motto Annuit Coeptis allude to the many signal interpositions of providence in favor of the American cause. Annuit Coeptis is translated as "He (God) has favored our undertakings,"* and *Wikipedia* adds: "*Annuit Coeptis* and ... *Novus Ordo Seclorum*, can both be traced to lines by the Roman poet Virgil. *Annuit Coeptis* comes from the *Aeneid*, book IX, line 625, which reads, *Iuppiter omnipotens, audacibus adnue coeptis*. It is a prayer by Ascanius, the son of Aeneas: "*Jupiter Almighty, favor [my] daring undertakings.*" According to the ancient state religion of Rome, properly called the Cultus Deorum Romanum, Jupiter was head of the pantheon of Gods." So, even in 1782 the Fathers of Our Country were not thinking Roman Republic, but Roman Empire.

[3] My learned friend Carl Conrad notes that Aeschylus, in a choral ode from *Agamemnon*, refers to Ares, God of War, as "money-changer of corpses": *ho chrysamoibos d' Ares somaton*. Some people think the Trojan War was a global deal. As for Melville's Confidence Man, gene-studies identify his father as Moby Dick, his son as a Robber Baron, and most Congressmen and Presidents as descendants.

[4] See John Perkins, *Confessions of an Economic Hit Man* (Penguin, 2006), *passim*. He claims to have been trained as undercover operative to ruin the economies of countries in the Middle East and South America on behalf of U.S. and international corporations collaborating with U.S. intelligence and governmental managers for this purpose, and tells in considerable detail how this was planned and carried out.

[5] *Encyclopædia Britannica, Micropædia III*, p. 709

LIVING IN THE HOLY LAND

Commissioned for and read at the Lewis and Clark Bicentennial Commemoration, under the Gateway Arch on the Mississippi River Front, St. Louis, September 23, 2006.

Forty score and seven years ago,
give or take a few Heavenly Days,
our Osage forebears brought forth,
on this continent, a new nation,
conceived in liberty and dedicated to
the proposition that all beings are created equal.

We had come down from the starry heavens
into this holy land, and we met here the mighty
Middle Waters, rolling evermore,
the Waters who come down from the Mountains of the West
and the Mountains of the East
and the Great Lakes of the North,
who move continually into the great
Waters of the South: we met them here,
the waters who make clean this Middle Earth,
the moving waters at their priest-like task
of pure ablution round earth's human shores,

and when we met, *Wi-zhin,* our *Elder Brother,* said,

Here stands Wah-shah-she,
whose body is the waters of the earth,

and the Water spoke to our people
in the liquid tones of a bird, saying,

O Little Ones,
if you make your bodies of me,
it will be difficult for death to overtake you,
and you will make clean and purify
all that comes to you. When I come from
my home in the sky to make
the flowers grow, Grandfather will paint
your face with many colors,
and smile upon the Little Ones.

When we heard this, our *Elder Brother* turned,
and we spoke together, saying,
Now our people shall be called
Wah-zhah-zhe, *we shall become*
the Ni-U-Kon-Ska, *People of the Middle Waters.*

We sent ahead, then, our messengers,
who traveled through three valleys, that were not valleys,
and in the fourth valley we met
those other great beings, of whom also
we made our bodies, so that we might live
to see old age, and live into
the Blessed Days, *Hom-ba Tha-gthin*:
the strong older beings of Earth and Water and Sky
who taught us how to live in the holy land:
beings among whom we established
our sacred center and set up there
our House of Mystery; beings who gave our sacred names,
the Mountain Lion, the Golden Eagle,
the Cedar Tree, the Deer, Black Bear
and Thunder and the others of our clans; beings whom we then set
in heavenly order around each earthly place
where we dwell, where we dance,
where we give names, deliberate and counsel,
where we decide on war or peace,
where those of us in need are given food and medicine.

HO-E-GA,

we named our center, meaning this earth that was
made to be habitable by separation from the water, meaning
this camp of our people when ceremonially pitched,
meaning this life proceeding from all the powers of all
the cosmic beings:

we set our lodges in concentric rings and kept
an order in our towns, we made
our community of Sun and Stars and Earth
and Waters, a Nation meant to move like them,
always in good ways, in lasting order,
so when we dance and when we sing we mean

a harmony like those of Sun and Stars and of
the always moving Waters,
the circle of the years and times, the circle of
the always living beings in this universe:
we give our children names so they may join
and move with us in this our dance,
while in their names and in our songs our story
will stay alive and say: we are *Wazhazhe*,
those who have names, those who give names,
those who are the nation
we have become.

*And yet, ten score and three years ago,
a great change came,*
it was brought home to us that *here
we had no continuing habitation:* a French dictator in Paris
had sold to a Virginia slaveowner in Washington
this holy land with all its Middle Waters.

Soon after, there passed by here the first few scouts
of many millions on their way
to the Pacific's golden shores.

We sent our messengers to Jefferson under
the Stars and Stripes, they traveled
with Chouteau as our friend, and they saw Jefferson,
a powerful and mysterious being:
he met our messengers, called himself their father,
promised we would be friends,
but would not let our friend Chouteau
be made our Agent. He named instead
the Redhead, William Clark,
who made an offer we could not refuse, and turned
Missouri into a state of slaves. So, our Diaspora began,
the young Republic's presidents had crossed
the Mississippi like the Rubicon and soon, like Augustus Caesar,
they ruled an Empire, while we moved on into
a western place, *by whose waters we sat down and set our Drum
under a willow arbor, and we wept,
remembering Missouri even as we sang.*

Then their Empire fought
a great Civil War between their North and South,
with us between them, shot and robbed by both,
and when that war was done the squatters came,
the swarming masses came on iron roads and killed
the buffalo and stole our corn and fouled the river where
we drank and bathed, and they and the Great White Father
and Sherman's Army said that land was theirs, so we
must move again—and so we did: we walked our trail
of tears into the Indian Territory and there
we made new centers for our bands,
we found new visions, and with the buffalo gone
the Longhorns came, and we let them fatten on our prairies,
we set our lodges along Bird Creek and along Salt Creek
and we survived and sang,
survived with song: we lost our elders, lost our ceremonies,
yet we brought back the Drum, with Kaw and Ponca help
we sang again.

And then the Oil Men came,
their rivers of black liquid gold washed away
too many of our people, too many of our ways,

the Oil Men made us rich they said,
and the rivers of Oil, the rivers of
Firewater and of Money, almost washed us away,

yet every year we sing, we set the Drum
at the sacred Center of the holy land,
and we dance to stay alive, with all
our footsteps prayers, with feathers in our moving fans
and on our moving bodies
to help our songs rise up to Wahkontah
that we may live, that we may yet remain
a sovereign Nation in this holy land.

WHAT THE EAGLE FAN SAYS

I strung dazzling thrones   of thunder beings
on a spiraling thread   of spinning flight,
beading dawn's blood   and blue of noon
to the gold and dark   of day's leaving,
circling with Sun   the soaring heaven
over turquoise eyes   of Earth below,
her silver veins,   her sable fur,
heard human relatives   hunting below
calling me down,   crying their need
that I bring them closer   to Wakonda's ways,
and I turned from heaven   to help them then.
When the bullet came,   it caught my heart,
the hunter's hands   gave earth its blood,
loosed our light beings,   let us float
toward the sacred center   of song in the drum,
but fixed us first   firm in song-home
that green light-dancers   gave to men's knives,
ash-heart in hiding where   deer-heart had beat,
and a one-eyed serpent   with silver-straight head
strung tiny rattles   around white softness
in beaded harmonies   of blue and red—
lightly I move now   in a man's left hand,
above dancing feet   follow the sun
around old songs   soaring toward heaven
on human breath,   and I help them rise.

Notes to **What the Eagle Fan Says**:

"What the Eagle Fan Says," uses the Old English "riddle" form, in which a being speaks of its deeper meanings and mysteries. Riddles were expected to use farfetched figures of speech: here, the eagle describes how it circles in the heavens as a bead-worker's needle circles in sewing beads onto white buckskin, around and around on the handle of an eagle-feather fan; and as a dancer circles the drum with fan in hand. The beaded handle's colors are scarlet of dawn, gold of noon, and midnight blue: these are the colors of a Gourd Dancer's blanket. Circling, the eagle pierces white clouds—thrones of thunder beings—as a needle pierces white buckskin. The feathers remain alive in the fan, whose motion sends up the prayers of dancers and singers for life to continue and the journey to be a good one.

The Country's

                    not quite all field
           or fence, blackberries root
      wild on stony soil
             among scrub timber, their
    thorn-vines stiff in winter where booted feet thrash
              through hip-high hay brown and stemmy after
      the dogs and rabbits running blind
to blackberry briars until they
            grab and tear them, saying
   this ground is taken for
           the smaller nations who live
      BENEATH, who perch BETWEEN—
surviving too spring's burnings with the wind swinging
             its gold-crackling scythe across
      the meadow, purging
   old nests and vines among rock-croppings
              as dried cow-chips go smoking
 back to the sky or floating
         creekwards with rains and leave
the marginal things such black
               clarity to grow in, where wild
   plums whiten, chokecherries bloom
              along winding gullies,
   new shoots spring green and fork
the air like snaketongues coming out
             of eggs to flicker tasting—
                the vines flower loosely
    when sunburn days move in
       and bare feet grow tough enough to walk
among thorn fringes on the way down
             to the low-water bridge, the
  rock-riffles and pool darkshining
 under arch of elms like a water-floored
         cathedral where brown
             naked bodies poise, then
 fly on the ropeswing down

                    from their high bank and skim with
                       one heel and rise up, up, to
                    drop through topwater's warmth into brown
             darkness, the spring-cold upwellings like waving
                          tendrils around the thighs—
                                 and July—
     July is *berries*,
                       the heaping pans
     and handled buckets spilling their black shining
                   with some a tight
                                   red still—
              and the reaching fingers stung
           by a hidden wasp to swell
                             like soft cucumbers are consoled
            by cobblers, whose thick doughs and crusts purple
              with juice and flake with sugar under yellow spilling
            of Jersey cream into blackpurple berries that taste
                           like nothing else,
                       waiting in roadside ditches,
                          rockpiles, woodmargins,
                       free between their thorns.

GO TO COLLEGE

Back about 1971 or 1972 I wrote something about teaching, and later added a beginning that morphed it into a piece about leaving the Rez and going off to "teach." Anno 2011, it looks pretty naïve: nothing about racism and brutal history, only mentions the difficulties inevitable in trying to move with a classroom-full of students through the winged words of poems or other texts, trying not to squash the meanings or smash the metaphoric wings as we passed. The ideal would be to have those word-wings settle onto an iris (flower or eye) and drink the nectar of meaning; the reality was more often squashing and smashing than nectar-sipping. This piece finally got printed in Mick Gidley's guest-edited issue of the British journal STAND that came out in December 2008. At least it reminds me that the resistance to classroom learning/teaching is strong, even within a mono-culture. I wonder how far back the hominid gene for argufying over sent messages kudzued into and over our brains.

                                      that's what he said,
                    my grandfather, when I
                        was eleven.
                        I-ko-eh,
                        Wi-tsi-go,
                        tha-gthin ge non-shka-hi—**
so I walked off into the groves
            of Academe.
                      That classroom teaching had me
          walking barefoot over the squishy
     caterpillar words on a page while keeping
                          one eye on those dancing tiger
        swallowtail meanings, and then
driving into a flock of them always smashing yellow
            fuzz on the windshield just as they
            would whisk into focus
          and always
                   thinking
of the flutter and stillness on some opened iris as
            they did reach
                      the nectar.

***Grandmother, Grandfather, I chose the good way (a ritual phrase)*

NOVEMBER 1988 IN WASHINGTON D.C.

      The guards are *friendly* when you walk
  at night up toward the Capitol, standing floodlit
         white and shining above
            its Roman pillars—
  "Good evening, where are you folks from?"
     "Ah, St. Louis—we live there."
           "Faan-TAS-tic!"—
      but there's an interruption,
a siren and a flashing cop-car swirling up
  through the parking lot behind two lost
      cars filled with tourist families
        —or maybe terrorists?
   But then the cars stop, the cop's
  lights stop flashing, there's a *friendly*
palaver and they swing around and drive
      out down the street,
and the young *friendly* guard, mustached,
  in black gloves and overcoat, who has
    been watching us and them, pounds
his gloved hands and says again *"FanTASTic!"* in a way
   that means he's checked us out, so we
      walk on, around the Capitol
and down dark steps and sidewalk to the
     Reflecting Pool—it must be
      several acres of still and
      shimmering dark alive
  with streetlights, brilliant green
and red of traffic signals, tail-lights's Red Glare—
  and then, from its other side, we see
the white unreal dome of the Capitol in it,
pointing down, down, at a star glittering deep
    in the pool below it, a large bright
    star—Venus, we think. At the moment,
this most powerful building in the world's
       asleep in Xanadu
  (a little water clears us of our deeds),
  a Pleasure Dome where people

—Chinese? Japanese?—are setting up their cameras now
to capture Pool and Capitol in one silver-bullet shot.
We could walk further, down the Mall,
and past the National Gallery where
they've captured Veronese's paintings for a time—
or by the Space Museum, where Astronauts
are dummies in their capsules, and
sleek missile-launchers stand like Michaels *waiting*
to shoot down Time for us
(they also served)—
or past the Smithsonian, where (I'm told)
the symbols of our Osage people wait, that let
us come down from the stars to form
a nation, here.
Instead, the night being damp, we turn
and walk on back along East Capitol, past
some trash receptacles on whose dull orange, painted
in yellow profile, is a *Redskin*—
RE-located from the *Buffalo Nickel*—
and now *PRESIDENT* over
the old news of this 1988 election, as we
walk eastward, into the full
and orange moon.

Parading with the Veterans of Foreign Wars

It interests me very much that a lot of American Indians have taken part in American wars as a way of showing support of the nation which has become the official guardian of Indian peoples. People say Indians are the most active of all American "ethnic groups," percentagewise, in wars of the 20th and 21st centuries.

It's one way to survive, after all. For a long time, military service has seemed to offer entry into the American "mainstream"—just as in the Roman Empire, citizenship could be obtained by being a member of a Roman Legion, even if you were a Gaul or Dalmatian or Iberian or whatever. My fullblood Osage Uncle Kenneth Jump served for instance in the Pacific campaigns of World War Two, and was active later in the Pawhuska (Osage) post of the American Legion, serving as Commander for a time. When I was given my Osage name in 1952, the feast and handgames and dance were held, I think, in the American Legion Hall there in Pawhuska.

Years later in St. Louis—about 1978—members of our Indian Community took part, one spring, in a parade organized in support of the Veterans of Foreign Wars. We had lately formed a St. Louis Indian Center and begun putting on powwows, and a lot of our dancers and singers were war-veterans. The Powwow is a way of survival: a form of lasting communal action by which to recover our place, which otherwise would have been taken away by the Empire. Dancing, singing, writing are among the more peaceful ways to reclaim our place. Cliff Walker, the Omaha chair of our St. Louis Powwow Committee, was a WW2 veteran who had for thirty years worked at the U.S. Army's Supply center in St. Louis, and many of our Indian Community people were veterans of WW2, of Korea, of Vietnam.

So when the local chapter of Veterans of Foreign Wars invited us to take part, to bring a kind of float to their parade, we were glad to be asked. One of our Community members had access to a big flatbed truck, and our local Drum with some of our dancers and women in their outfits—Gourd Dance, "straight," "traditional" and "fancy wardance" regalia, and the women in shawls and maybe white buckskin—rode on the flatbed, while the rest of us in our outfits walked behind the men. Those on the flatbed held up a big banner announcing our Indian Center Powwow to be held that June in Jefferson Barracks Park, in south St. Louis.

That park, as mentioned in the poem, is where the United States Dragoons were quartered for the Indian Wars beginning in the 1830's. A great many veterans are buried there from the various wars from then to now, and starting with World War One a considerable number of these are American Indians. Our early powwows were held on other grounds, and it gave real satisfaction when some of our Indian Community people with friends in the Park Service were able to talk the Jefferson Barracks people into letting us dance there.

There was a fair amount of reluctance based on the perception of Indians as radical AIM members prone to violence, or alcoholic troublemakers in general. The general view I sensed among people I dealt with over the years—particularly when I once had to persuade Washington University people to let us hold a mini-powwow using Missouri Humanities money in a university building—is that Indians are apt to leave a big mess, being dirty and slovenly and obviously just a poorer class of people: why else would they live in such appalling conditions on their Reservations, or come into the City and be so irresponsibly poor and helpless?

So to dance in the green and pleasant confines of Jefferson Barracks Park, overlooking the great rolling Mississippi, under pines and tulip and sweetgum and oak trees, with room for the traders' booths and for the visiting Indian families from Arizona and New Mexico and Oklahoma and Kansas and Nebraska and the Dakotas, maybe down from Wisconsin and up from Mississippi and Louisiana, over from Illinois and Indiana—that was a kind of sweet survival statement by those against whom the Dragoons had made war to cleanse the Manifestly Destined United States of our kind forever.

And of course the rest of the poem is very close to how it was. It is almost a "found poem," because it simply reports what we did and what took place. But I thought it carried a good deal of resonance, and it has seemed to wake up some of my academic friends in a gentle way.

Apache, Omaha, Osage, Choctaw,
                       Comanche, Cherokee, Oglala, Micmac:
our place was ninety-fifth,
and when we got there with our ribbon shirts
and drum and singers on the trailer,
women in shawls and traditional dresses,
we looked into the muzzle of
an Army howitzer in front of us.

"Hey, Cliff," I said,
"haven't seen guns that big
since we were in Wounded Knee."
Cliff carried the new American flag
donated by another post; Cliff prays
in Omaha for us, being chairman
of our Powwow Committee, and his prayers

keep us together, helped
by hard work from the rest of course.
"They'll move that one-oh-five ahead," Cliff said.
They did, but then the cavalry arrived.
No kidding, there was this troop outfitted
with Civil War style uniforms and carbines,
on horseback, metal clopping on
the asphalt street, and there
on jackets were the insignia:
the Seventh Cavalry, George Custer's bunch.

"Cliff," Walt said, "they think you're Sitting Bull."
"Just watch out where you're stepping, Walt,"
Cliff said, "Those pooper-scoopers
will not be working when the parade begins."
"Us women walking behind the trailer
will have to step around it all
so much, they'll think we're dancing,"
was all that Sherry said.

We followed
the yellow line, and here and there
some fake war-whoops came out to us
from sidewalk faces, but applause
moved with us when the singers started,
and we got our banners seen announcing
this year's Pow-Wow in June,
free to the public in Jefferson Barracks Park—
where the Dragoons were quartered for the Indian Wars.

When we had passed the ***Judging Stand***
and pulled off to the little park all
green and daffodilly under the misting rain,
we put the shawls and clothing in the cars
and went back to the Indian Center, while
Cliff and George Coon went out and got
some chicken from the Colonel *(Sanders)*
that tasted great, given the temporary
absence of buffalo here in the
Gateway to the West, St. Louis.

OUTSIDE IN ST. LOUIS

Walking through the door
           is easy when it is your home—
     but then, how many doors
   belong to you? In time,
     none,
            except the one where it turns dark
    and timeless. —But
         it keeps us entertained, the sidewalk does,
with lighted windows, spring flowers
            and autumn leaves, playthings of children
  to walk around, step over—left
              at dinner time to go inside to smells of
  food and dancing pictures
           on television screens; and here,
                      outside,
    the pigeons tilt above me on their way
         to find loose grain in a feedstore loft:
           two, with
   rainbows on their necks, descend to
 waddle and peck
      at ash wings in the gutter. What,
I wonder, do they fly through,
           among,
              within? Me,
     I hear the traffic, step
  with caution from the curb—
              they, inside the whisper of
a soft St. Louis rain, may hear
       The ocean speaking: not just the long swells that lash
Pacific shores, but those that boom
              on Hatteras, commune on their
subhuman channels with these pigeons' minds;
       maybe the rumbling of Colorado thunderstorms
forecasts for them this weekend's weather—
          even through rainclouds, light is polarized to
  brilliantine their way; and though
      their way back into everlasting spring's
   not lighted up, as for
  the tiny migrant warblers who fly the Atlantic non-stop,

               by star-maps glittering in the
                    molecules of their genes, their history
               is packed, rainproof and portable,
     in sperm and ova, even
                    the lodestone that they home with's just
                         a speck of ferrite in their brain—
          my God, these rock-doves make
      from our crumbs a feast, our windowsills
                         their trysting-places, set their pullulating
     nests into dark empty places warmed by
                              our wasted heat:
The Outside is
                their home, its door the wind, sidewalks just
                         angelic parking lots—
                                        So when they do
          come spiraling down to sidewalks with
                    their *Aphrodisiac* sigh of wings, I hear
               Her giggling as
     they strut and coo: *She* lets them love it on
                                        the outside of
                    the street's many doors,
          as I remind myself in passing daily over
               the hard concrete within our here and now
                    into some other space and time.

GIVEN
—for the children

this world to grow into, I know
they'll repossess it shortly, along with
what's left of me—yet, rumpled
into this little pocket
of time, I wish
there were a little more of me to sing
the mortgage payments—how it really
dawns on me this morning as
the light has brimmed and spills all rosy into
the east with robins paying
their rent in song and with the downy
woodpecker's telephone-pole tattoo explaining
the nod of daffodils and endless
pinoaks, maples, ash and sycamore and locusts,
sweetgum dogwood and redbud bowing into the April
windstream over
us blind and flightless creatures blundering
noisy and slow as brachiosaurs, squeaking and rumbling
like humpback whales beneath quick birds where they
are singing that the springing wealth of new
leaves and light and flowers has made it
practical to consummate the mystery of
nesting, if
within earshot the right females would return
the secret signs that they will partner them.
We see, we *learn*
to see and hear and feel, the way
those leaves come out of buds all tight
with liquid virtue rising from earth-blind roots
into bright air to fan
their soft translucent green as
they ask the light into their bowers
of sugars, starches, lignins, as we see
in green and hear in song how light
becomes a tree and holds
the singers in its branches where curving
and blue as sky small eggs will open
and blind reptilian robins fledge and find how
to sing the light back into dawn,

their arias and duets soaring above starsongs
of tree-frogs in the summer dark, just as
into translucent salmon sunrise the stars
dissolve, white clouds set sail across
the blue dazzle above us walking on
our stony earth where clopping
and grating we look up into
those heavens of green and blue and white where the trees
without moving are given the earth and
the sun and the stars, and those who have wings now
are singing and those who have climbed
from sea to earth and air and live now on dew and the tree's
plenty are singing, where the moon brings back
a softer light from the sun, where the stars bring us the great
glittering darkness that has no end.

OVER BY FAIRFAX, LEAVING TRACKS

    The storm's left
           this fresh blue sky, over
  Salt Creek running brown
and quick, and a huge tiger
      swallowtail tasting the brilliant
  orange flowers beside our trail.
Lightning and thunder've spread
  a clean sheet of water over
these last-night possum tracks
  straight-walking like a dinosaur in
      soft mud, and next to these we've
left stippled tracks from soles made
    in Hong Kong, maybe with Osage oil.
      Lawrence and Wesley pick blue-speckled flints
along our path, one Ponca boy
      in braids, one Osage
    in cowboy hat.
            Over the blue Pacific, green Atlantic we
have come together here: possum's
the oldest furred being in this New World,
      we're newest in his Old World.
Far older, though,
  and younger too, a tiger swallowtail has
    gone sailing from those orange flowers over
          to sky-blue nectar: the wild morning
   glories
will spring up where she's touched, marking
        her next year's trail.
  Makes me wonder,
  if archaeologists should ever dig these prints
   with possum's here, whether they'll see
the winged beings who moved
    in brightness near us, leaving no tracks except
    in flowers and
   these winged words.

Two Riddles: A Diptych

The Swan's Song
Old English: from The Exeter Book

Garbed in silence   I go on earth,
dwell among men   or move on the waters.
Yet far over halls   of heroes in time
my robes and the high   air may raise
and bear me up   in heaven's power
over all nations.   My ornaments then
are singing glories,   and I go in song
bright as a star,   unstaying above
the world's wide waters,   as a wayfaring soul.

Drone with Hellfire Missiles
Iraq, Afghanistan, Gaza, Libya

From soot I rise: bright red my eye,
Night-black my body: bat-wings rigid,
Sharp gold-wired brain   aware and circling,
I beam the phantom   faces up
Of families who sit   sipping sweet coffee,
Set them in a cannon's   unseen cross-hairs,
Small moving creatures   marked for death.

EARTH AND DIAMONDS

How far from truth to beauty, say
in diamonds?
Can we make either out of facts
put flatly, crunched together so their facets
crack light and spill
its rainbows over earth the way
plain carbon does when it is crushed into
a diamond, say?
A scientific fact was once
that stars made diamonds by their heavenly
"influence" acting deep within
the earth, mutating gunk
into bright gems;
but now it is a fact of science that earth
composes diamonds of itself—
and yet the earth itself was made
in superstars (another fact
of science, for the moment),
so that the house which stars once built
still crystallizes in the shape of stars, still
shines like them,
in language anyhow.

Of course
(you say) the earth, this common place, can't really shine.
But that's because we live too close to it:
the astronauts have seen
our muddy planet shine,
a blue star up in heaven.
That's what their eyes have seen:
their minds, of course, know very well it's not
a fact that's pure, it has
a flaw, depending on your point of view. It's air
that shines, and water mostly, earth
just holds these shining facts around
its heavy darkness.

So flights of angels, passing through our bodies,
may see a neutron shine
gemlike with facets, all the points of
inner structure netting
the radiant waves and fishing out
their rainbow messages of peace
from the God of Storms.
That, you'll say, is not
a fact—but if we just remove
the angels and insert
a physicist, you may allow
it is a fact though medaled
with metaphors and circumcised
by adjectives: yes,
our physicist might say,
it is a fact
that neutrons have a structure,
and perhaps that each is like
a crystal, certainly
neutrons are being probed by beams of
some other particles,
and in the spectrum which comes back to us
from deep inside these specks of space
are messages concerning Universal
Creation and Apocalypse.

Thus far we state pure facts, although
they are imperfect when they're packed into
the seedy figures of our speech,
and blossom only in the arabesques
of math, which has no fruitful symbols for
Creation and Apocalypse except
a change of signs.

—*FACTUS* meant *SOMETHING MADE*, in Roman mouths,
then English let it take the place of *TRUTH*.
Shakespeare was called, by Robert Greene,
"an absolute *FACTOTUM* in his own conceit."

He did it all,
that is, he *MADE* it all; instead of acting,
Shakespeare began to make the forms
for others's actions: yes, FACTOTUM,
that's the word.

People make diamonds now from coal, as easily
as they make perfume out
of oil, or pantyhose
from tar—
but diamonds we make
just as volcanoes did, with heat and pressure,
just as volcanoes were themselves
created by the moving
continents where the ocean's crust
dives under and the mountain-ship
floats over and begins to burn and thunder,
creating atmosphere, sunsets,
and diamonds in time.

And the male bird of paradise creates his bower.
to woo a mate, in fact the blue one chooses
only blue things to put in his,
he even mixes blue
paint and spreads it on his
bower's wall, using a piece of wood
or other brush to spread
the paint he's made from berries and
his way of seeing things.

But then, the fact is that
when once his mate is mated there
she leaves and builds her nest
and lays her eggs up in
some ordinary tree, and he just lets her go,
he takes no interest in the mortgage or the weather or the eggs, or in
those rising generations at their song,

he paints just what he sees, he makes
his gemlike house
of blue lights, keeps the species special and himself
fit to survive—and he's
a dinosaur, it seems, with warm blood, one
who put on feathers and survived: or so
facticians now assert as fact: the birds,
as Michael Castro says, are *DYNA-SOARS!*

If that is fact, we can no longer
believe that dinosaurs became extinct, just as we can
no longer hold that earth, not stars,
composes diamonds.

The trouble is, we keep exploding facts
into old myths, and then compressing myths
into new facts—
and so, in this dark kaleidoscope
of headlined findings, what once was
crystal clear becomes too nebulous
to be believed—
yet then becomes the evidence
that speaks of how our universe evolved,
as do the nebulae in space that once
were "clouds" and now are "ghosts"
of superstars that still broadcast the news
of brilliant bowers painted
upon the heavens long before
there was an earth
to sparkle bluely like a diamond in
the sky and
               make us wonder,
O twinkling little fact, just WHAT
you are: if true, how beautiful,
if beautiful, how true.

GEODE

I still remember ocean, how
she came in with all I wanted, how we opened
the hard shell we had made
of what she gave me and painted into
that lodge's white walls the shifting
rainbows of wave-spray—
I remember even the vague drifting
before the shell was made, my slow swimming
amidst the manna until I sank
down into stone, married, rooted there, joined
its stillness where the moving waters
would serve us as the moon would bring them by.
Growing, I remember how softness
of pale flesh secreted the smooth hardness
of shell, how the gritty pain
was healed with rainbow tears
of pearl,
I remember dreaming
of the new creatures flying through air
as the sharks swam through ocean
hallucinating feathers and dinosaurs,
pterodactyls and archæopteryxes,
great turquoise dragonflies
hovering, shimmering, hawking after the huge
mosquitoes fat with brontosaurus blood. And when
I died and the softness vanished inside
my shell and the sea flowed in I watched
it drying as the waters ebbed, saw how my bony whiteness held
at its heart the salty gel whose desire swelled
and grew and globed against the limey mud,
chalcedony selving edged and spiked its way
through dreams of being flowers trembling
against the wind, snowflakes falling
into a desert spring. But the rain
of limestone hardened round us and my walls
grew full of holes, I waked into
a continent of caves, a karst-land where

sweet water chuckled and trickled, siliceated through
my crevices as once the salty ocean had, and I felt
purple quartz-crystals blossom where
my pale flesh had been.
Then I knew my dream
was true, and I waited for
the soft hand to come down through my dream
and lift me into sunlight, give me there to diamond
saws that sliced me in two, to diamond dust that polished
my new selves of banded agate,
I let them separate and shelve them heavy
on either side of a word-hoard whose light leaves
held heavy thoughts between
the heavier, wiser, older lines of all
my mirrored selves, the wave-marks left
by snowflake-feathery amethyst
ways of being,
                                      by all those words,
by the Word, made slowly,
slowly, in-
                to Stone.

TRANSFIGURATIONS
December, 1992: the day Ronald Reagan addressed the Oxford Union
December, 2002: after Tony Blair supported Bush's plan to attack Iraq

1.
Depressing, depressing—they found him,
says the happy mother of
the bright and decent Oxford students
who've just been listening to Ronnie, just
had tea and wine and canapés or what not with him,
—they found him utterly charming, and his speech
to the Oxford Union audience smoothly
reminded them how special
Anglo and American relations are,
how we've stood together
against the Nazis and the Commies, how
the Evil Empire's now collapsed
because the Iron Lady stood with him and now
the Tories can get on with wrecking
the National Health Service and bring back—
oh hell, it's too disgusting
and tedious to go through. And yet—
Could they be right? this bristly Maggie
and smooooth Ronnie, who sent hit men to bomb,
torture and murder in Honduras,
Northern Ireland, Nicaragua, Guatemala,
El Salvador—might Polly-Scientists paint
their blood-stained work as necessary
and therefore beautiful and
good, like Andrew Jackson's Trail of Tears
or battles won in France by Henry Fifth?
A question much too big for this Nobody.

So I'm
just standing here in Oxford,
here on the Turl, looking
at gorgeous Italian ties, these brilliant silks
in Walter's of the Turl, to brighten up
the rainy, flooding weather of this day—
early December at the end
of Michaelmas Term when the brown
roiling Cherwell has risen up

almost into the Botanical Gardens: I'm hoping
the Oxford Union's merely as stupid
as I recall its being in the Fifties, though not so dumb
as Parliaments, or Presidents, in the Eighties.

2.
Looking at bright silks in a dark mood, though,
I stand here
window shopping only
to keep from thinking how the rich men rule.
They're NOT immortal, thank God.
Babylon burns, its Emperor slips
into Alzheimer's, lion and lizard keep
the ruins where once Belshazzar slept, their silks
and satins flitter on clothes-moth wings—
old Presidents tumble in the add-bleach cycle,
rich advisors rot on compost-heaps,
decay in footnotes.
Still, they return like Terminators, they
recycle and repeat their wars: if only
death WERE the mother of beauty—
famished caterpillars feasting
on poison-packed leaves and turning them into
waving angelic wings, Monarch
and Luna Moth and Tiger Swallowtail.
But those fly free, while fat silk-moths must never
come forth, must never rasp
and ruin the one long thread they spin into their shroud, never
visit moon-shadowed flowers, like wingless deities must die
to robe us in raw silk and let the chemists
conjure from coal angelic glories, tweak
oil-films from fossil seas and set them
dancing in rainbow swirls upon
a dandy's ties—
called up from time
by Chinese women, German chemists, by old Englishwomen winding,
unwinding—those "silkwives"
of fifteenth century London—careful as Urania with
that Phoenix-egg of the rainbow-winged
first universe when from her great

brooding song this universe
exploded into brilliant quarks
that cooled into space and time and stars within each
infinite pupil—
flashing, darkening to matter, digesting
self to blossom where
in the Emperor's Masque his minions dance,
mirrored in silken brilliance, sleek in
crimson pajamas, black satin sheets of bordello,
a fop's foulard, silk of Q. C.'s robes—
thread twisting and turning,
spinning, weaving, O dark
Mother of Bright Wings—where genies glide
in silken gravity of water down
the turbine-wheel, becoming electric
current alive with song-ghosts, old sand dunes melted
to sapphire silicon, rare earth awakened in
germanium touching golden wires
to music of Apollonian lyres—and **see**
how Psalms of David melt
by Christian alchemy into stained glass
of Placebo and Dirige, Jerubbabel
channels old Babylon into
New Jerusalem, bright faces passing over
the glass of Siloa's brook that flows
fast by the Oracle of God, spirits stepping out onto
the Thames, the Hudson, Amazon, Volga, Hwang-ho—
and far off, see the glittering Stars
and Galaxies drop into
a Black Hole as dead leaves go
into a bonfire, disembodied
to flame, ashes, smoke and light and heat,
but then become
the springing flowers—trees—grapes and
wine, apples and brandy—world into words,
speech into Book, Songs into Drum—
wrenched down history's
Black Holes into an insurrection
of Dark Matter, Quasar dying
as from decaying Space and Time arise
to fly away new Bubble Worlds, brief rainbow minds upon

their film of bursting time—
O see
this great and vibrant world become
the tiny set of words upon
a baby's tongue
and how it grows, how all that old debris
from superstars becomes this mass of
proteinated sense and memory, foetus that
coheres to selfhood, *"crying for the light,
and with no language but a cry."*

—Yet still THEY'LL say, they always say—the Presidents
and would-be Kings, clanking their mind-chains—
*We work for greater good, we do it all
entirely for true Peace and Freedom, for
the Empire, for
America, the Beautiful*—
those children that we starved, exploded, those whom
we burnt in the idol Petrol's belly, whom
we sacrificed to our Old Glory
that's waving down here on
our Humvee bumpers, high up on our mighty
impregnable skyscrapers: everywhere
in the rocket's red glare
our flag is still there.

3.
Well then, a sunset walk in this curious universe,
leaving in their windows
those mothwing ties, leaving to Heaven
one dozing forgetful President with Counselor Maggie,
that brisk Attila the Hen—

much brighter, out here on the galactic rim
of Oxford, walking with my light of life,
la Stella mia, given a timeless
evening translucence here to walk through, all
these WATERY trans-figurings,
Port Meadows on the fringe of Oxford as the

Cherwell floods them, sunset drowsy on
their momentary pools—
seeing the lapwings wheel and dive among the
white gulls swirling, black rooks pubbing, magpies plotting,
men sitting pipe in mouth, long rods across canal, waiting
for a fish to pull the rod-tip down, between
canal boats where a pair of serene swans
now sail grandly across to seize our bits
of bread from a baguette with ham and salad,
snap bits from fingers or spear chunks in
the water, fallen floating soggies gobbled by
coots, moorhens and ducks as we stride by, passing
the waterlogged Meadow's wild
ponies shaggy for winter, one golden
palomino Arab trotting,
prancing for his rider, posting stiff-
spined in her billed cap—we walk through Wolvercote and turn
at last down toward The Trout Inn, beside
the stallion-muscling ripples of water under bridge and down
the weir, its swirls roilyboiling upon themselves, moiré
of satin moving, mothwing sunset slowly
spinning in eddies past
the people on the patio looking down.

—When we walked down through Jericho, so gentrified,
we saw the fluffy counterspy
cats, slinking into alleys, slipping beneath parked cars,
stepping disapproving on Dead Sea asphalt, plotting their
escapes to high window-seats where Persians calmly
look down from double-glazed Nirvana
on us in chilly Maya—silent as keepers of our bloody past encrypted
there in the National Register of Archives in Kew
among pools a-shiver with swans around
thousands of parchment corpses
from the Hundred Years' War, when English chivalry led
by merciless King Edward and his sons, the Black
Prince and his brothers, crossed
the Channel to rape, pillage and loot French villages:
those nunneries despoiled, the blind King of Bohemia slain,
those homicides come home to pardons for good service

in France by King's testimony, given
on Justice Itinerant rolls, beside each felony indictment
the mark of pardon, King's X, Pax—
Pardon Me For Murder, Your Majesty?
I DO: YOUR PRIVATE ENGLISH CRIMES ARE PARDONED
FOR PUBLIC MURDERS, DONE IN FRANCE FOR ME.

4.

—I know the Oxford swans still fly, they are not pinioned
like the black swans in London's St. James Park,
that royal park behind Zen Downing Street,
the War Office, Whitehall and all that. And yet,
"The silver swan, that living had no note . . .
More geese than swans now live, more fools than wise,"
and now, as we step down to the Trout Inn, small
arrows of geese zoom low overhead,
turn sharply and shoot southward
over the flooding Thames not far above
the broken walls of Godstow Nunnery,
God's Place beside its lock where the waters tremble,
stone and water winding around
each other a clear mauve
and steely silver sunset
where Venus glitters and a helicopter flutters,
mothlike glinting, maybe with Ronald Reagan returning
royally to America, pardoned by
the Oxford Student Union here beside *the chartered Thames*,
flying above Blake's vision of an England where,
serenely crimson on these mellow stones,
the hapless infant's sigh
runs in blood down college walls.

A Song That We Still Sing

On the way from Oklahoma up to the Sun Dance
at Crow Dog's Paradise on the Rosebud Sioux Reservation,
      they'd stopped a few minutes,
my Ponca cousins from Oklahoma—
      they were way out there by some kind
of ruins, on the August prairie,
      some kind of fort it may
have been, they stopped
      to eat a little, get out and
stretch their legs, the van
      had got too little for
      the kids and all.
           And they were walking
not paying much attention and they heard
      the singing and then Casey said,
      Listen, that's Ponca singing.
    Hear it? Where's it coming from?
They listened, and Mike said,
      Sounds like it's over
inside those walls or whatever
      they may be, over there.
           So they walked
through the dry short grass
      towards the raised earth walls
and up on them, and looked
inside that wide compound, and there
      was not a soul in sight.

That was a Wolf Song, Mike said.
Yes, a Victory Song, Casey said.

When they told me later, we looked and
decided that it was where the Cheyennes
and some of their allies had chased some troopers
      inside a fort and
      taunted them—
           after Sand Creek it was,
that time the news got out of what

     had been done to Black Kettle and
       his people there beneath
that big American flag which they'd been given
     in token that this peaceful band
       was not to be attacked,
   and then at dawn the Reverend Colonel
    Chivington and his men attacked and massacred
      some hundreds who could not escape—
       one small boy, running
    for refuge, was shot down at a hundred yards,
because, as Chivington had told his troops,
    Nits make lice. The women's breasts,
      sliced off, were made into
        tobacco pouches, as were the scrotums
of men. George Bent, a half-Cheyenne who was there,
       who'd been a Confederate soldier and
both wrote and spoke English and Cheyenne,
      has told about it in his letters—
       he saw White Antelope come out
     unarmed from his tepee, pointing up
  at Old Glory waving over the village there,
       then when the troopers kept on shooting,
he stood unmoved and sang, as they shot him down,
the death-song he'd composed for such a time:

     Nothing lives long
    except the earth and the mountains.

So I asked Casey and Mike,
     what do you think you heard, inside that place?
  —I guess, Mike said, up in Nebraska
    there must have been some Poncas
      who joined the Cheyennes there and fought
   the soldiers till they chased them
      into that fort.
  Then Casey said,
    We recognized that song. It's one
     that we still sing.

ESP Scan for 40th Birthday

I know that mind
        is only matter—
    but will someone please explain
           what matter IS?
In 1895, for instance, Roentgen
      quite accidentally saw that a screen
was fluorescing when his cathode-ray
        machine was on; he
    discovered X-rays thus, and so
        the concept *matter* had to be revised—
and still more radically shifted when, next year,
          Becquerel found his halides fogged
              by some invisible emanation
out of uranium ore, not sent by man.
      The problem is that down in my aging self
        I've got no phosphor screens,
    no silver halides,
        to let me know of such great accidents
          when things from outer space sweep
through this mind:
                of course,
      these wrinkles on my face tell something,
and language helps,
      its metaphors transpose
    invisible joy to visible love—see,
        like stones in ultraviolet darkness,
          faces of lovers luminesce,
their black silver smiles
        curving like Saturn's rings—
but most cloud-chambers of language
    are obsolete, they catch
      only what's looked for:
    the unimagined nectar goes through,
    and the tongue
        spits coffee-grounds.

But lately, I have thought of just
        the right sensitive receiver:
it is a wilderness, big enough
    to find a vision in
        while quite alone. So yesterday
I made my lot
      by not raking the lawn
and watching a two-year-old run
    through falling leaves—
and sure enough the message came, when he
    fell with them,
    and then got up,
and caught one in the air,
      a mulberry leaf that time
    had turned bright yellow
        with static-spots of rust.
I'll look tomorrow at how the birds fly dark
    against the snow,
and how snowflakes come sailing into focus
    before my windshield,
        and in the mirror how my beard turns white.
Or maybe later, when
    my SELF has cooled
        near absolute zero,
it will grow super-conductive,
like a helium-crystal laser, impossible and yet
        so sensitive that
touched by the **Gegenschein** it would
      flash out a Lazarus-light
on memory's moiré,
    and there would float into view
        the hologram of all my scattered days,
their storms contained as a brilliant play of things
    that meadows would understand as rain,
      stars as a zodiac of lightnings.

>But maybe light
>>is not the place to look: I know
>>>that as my deafness grows
>>>>to sounds that come through air,
>>vibrations through these bones
>come in always louder—
>>>and it may be my skull
>>is all the hope I have
>>>to place against the vibrant spheres
>>>>and hear them singing—
I used to put my head
>against a telephone pole
>>and hear the wires humming
down through the pole, never needing
>to tap their tightstrung copper to be in
>>on what was said across those miles
>of empty, blowing prairie
>>on the coldest winter day.

THE PRIME MINISTER EXPLAINS

"Did you ever," he said,
"wonder why you see so few
housefly corpses, other than those
you've swatted into smears?

Well, fact is that way back when,
a swarm of flies was on the wall and watched
the Bodily Assumption.
'Hey,' they said,
'No wings! Let's ask our Lord, maybe
He'll show us how it's done!'

So, I was out walking up and down a
golf course with two billionaires, working
on contracts for a minor war or two,
and here those little buzzers came
with their request—
'Please, Lord,' they said,
'We want Bodily Assumption, just before
we're swatted.'
"Simple," I said—I wanted to impress
the billionaires, who were trying
to negotiate a higher price per soul delivered—so
I gave the Big Oil Man one fly swatter,
and the Big Arms Man another, while
two flies got ready for the swatters—and just
as the swatters swung I snapped my fingers, and
ZOOP! The flies were way up in the heavens buzzing
happily ever after while the billionaires
were wondering how they missed.
They don't call me
Lord of the Flies for nothing,"
he said, and off
the whole bunch buzzed to swarm
all over babies' corpses during
the next two wars.

PREHISTORIC SURVEILLANCE IN BETHLEHEM?

Chaunteclere Has 100,000,000-Year-Old HD Curved-Screen 3D & Binocular Color TeleVision[1] inherited from his Grandpa, Tyrannosaurus Rex,[2] installed Behind His Third Eyelids[3] (Eco-friendly: No Batteries or Plug-in Needed). Several famous people are spinning cuckoons in their graves at this revelation: for instance, Geoffrey Chaucer,[4] William Shakespeare,[5] Henry Vaughan,[6] William Blake and Isaac Newton,[7] Pieter Breughel Jr,[8] and Karl Marx.[9]

> So three questions remain
> in this supernatural mystery:
> *What did Chaunteclere SEE,*
> *when did he see it,*
> > AND
> *do roosters crow in Heaven?*[10]

Notes to **Prehistoric Surveillance in Bethlehem**

(1) Since Chaunteclere has always lived in the light, his inherited condominium in Bethlehem uses color TV for round-the-clock surveillance. Adam and Eve, by fortunate fall, went 24/7 and daily walk in darkness, but have inward eyes.

(2) DNA from the fossilized femur of a Tyrannosaurus has been found to resemble most closely that of the domestic chicken. The reported comment on this from publicists for the *Kentucky Fried Chicken* franchise operators was, "What clucks we have been." A new ad campaign is reported to be in preparation, based on the theme *Our Customers Can Eat Them First.*

"The domestic chicken (*Gallus domesticus*) originally descended from the wild red jungle fowl (*Gallus gallus*) of southeastern Asia. The females, including mature hens and younger pullets, are raised for their edible eggs and meat. Immature males, called cockerels, are castrated to become meat birds called capons. Mature males, called cocks, or roosters, have long been used for sport" (Encyclopædia Britannica, 15th ed. [Micropædia 2.830]).

(3) *Here are excerpts from an article by Michael Purdy in the Washington University RECORD for the week of February 15, 2010:*

Researchers at Washington University School of Medicine in St. Louis have peered deep into the eye of the chicken and found a masterpiece of biological design. Scientists mapped five types of light receptors in the chicken's eye. They discovered the receptors were laid out in interwoven mosaics that maximized the chicken's ability to see many colors in any given part of the retina, the light-sensing structure at the back of the eye.

"Based on this analysis, birds have clearly one-upped us in several ways in terms of color vision," says Joseph C. Corbo, M.D., PhD, senior author and assistant professor of pathology and immunology and of genetics. "Color receptor organization in the chicken retina greatly exceeds that seen in most other retinas and certainly that in most mammalian retinas." Corbo plans follow-up studies of how this organization is established. He says such insights could eventually help scientists seeking to use stem cells and other new techniques to treat the nearly 200 genetic disorders that can cause various forms of blindness. [Kram YA, Mantey S, Corbo JC. Avian cone photoreceptors tile the retina as five independent, self-organizing mosaics. PLoS One, Feb. 1, 2010.]

Birds likely owe their superior color vision to not having spent a period of evolutionary history in the dark, according to Corbo. Birds, reptiles and mammals are all descended from a common ancestor, but during the age of the dinosaurs, most mammals became nocturnal for millions of years. Birds, now widely believed to be descendants of dinosaurs, never spent a similar period living mostly in darkness. As a result, birds have more types of cones than mammals.

"The human retina has cones sensitive to red, blue and green wavelengths," Corbo says. *"Avian retinas also have a cone that can detect violet wavelengths, including some ultraviolet, and a specialized receptor called a double cone that we believe helps them detect motion."* In addition, most avian cones have a specialized structure that Corbo compares to *'cellular sunglasses': a lens-like drop of oil within the cone that is pigmented to filter out all but a particular range of light.* Researchers used these drops to map the location of the different types of cones on the chicken retina. They found that the different types of cones were evenly distributed throughout the retina, but two cones of the same type were never located next to each other. "This is the ideal way to uniformly sample the color space of your field of vision," Corbo says. "It appears to be a global pattern created from a simple localized rule: you can be next to other cones, but not next to the same kind of cone."

Corbo speculates that extra sensitivity to color may help birds in finding mates, which often involves colorful plumage, or when feeding on berries or other colorful fruit.

"Many of the inherited conditions that cause blindness in humans affect cones and rods, and it will be interesting to see if what we learn of the organization of the chicken's retina will help us better understand and repair such problems in the human eye," Corbo says.

(4) Mr. Chaucer, speaking from the office of the scribe Adam Pynkhurst, where he was supervising Mr. Pynkhurst's efforts to revise the Hengwrt Manuscript and produce the Ellesmere Manuscript of the *Canterbury Tales,* referred reporters to what the Nun's Priest had said of Chaunteclere:

> *His voyce was merrier than the merry orgon*
> *On masse-dayes that in the churche gon.*
> *Wel sikerer was his crowing in his lodge*
> *Than is a clocke, or abbey orolodge.*
> *By nature he knew ech ascensioun*
> *Of the equinoxial in thilke toun;*
> *For whan degrees fiftene weren ascended,*
> *Thanne crewe he, that it myghte nat been amended.*

(5) Mr. Shakespeare tweeted his response to a reporter's question from New Place in Stratford, where he had lately retired: *"C Hamlet sc.1, Horatio/Bernardo/Marcellus re brd of dwnng sngth al nite lng."*

(6) Said Mr. Vaughan, "I told you so, in my poem Cock-Crowing, if you'll remember what I said about seeds of light:

> *Father of lights! what Sunnie seed,*
> *What glance of day hast thou confin'd*
> *Into this bird? To all the breed*
> *This busie Ray thou hast assign'd;*
> > *Their magnetism works all night,*
> > *And dreams of Paradise and light.*
>
> *Their eyes watch for the morning hue,*
> *Their little grain expelling night*
> *So shines and sings, as if it knew*
> *The path unto the house of light.*
> > *It seems their candle, howe'r done,*
> > *Was tinn'd and lighted at the sunne.*

(7) Mr. Newton, with much gravity, refused to comment, but Mr. Blake cheerfully pulled out a concertina borrowed from Allen Ginsberg and with its accompaniment chanted the final stanza of his *Mock On, Mock On, Voltaire, Rousseau:*

> *The atoms of Democritus*
> *And Newton's particles of light*
> *Are sands upon the Red Sea shore*
> *Where Israel's tents do shine so bright.*

(8) Mr. Breughel said, "You may recall that I painted Chaunteclere in Bethlehem on a stable roof, above which a great Star shone, from which a beam came directly down and into the eye of Chaunteclere where he was looking down at us from the roof above Mary and Joseph and the Child, before whom the Three Kings were standing or kneeling. He was there for a reason."

(9) Dr. Marx said: "I explained in the 1840s, as is reported in the *Eleventh Edition of the Encyclopedia Britannica* (volume 17, page 807), that the proletariat cannot emancipate itself except by breaking all the chains, by dissolving the whole constituted society, by recreating man as a member of the human society in the place of established states and classes. Then the day of German resurrection will be announced by the crowing of the Gallican cock." A Messianic prophecy, *nicht wahr?* out of the empty tomb, a spectre haunting Europe?

(10) For answers, stay tuned to research reports at ArchæoBLOGOS.ink.

LIBEL SUIT
CHAUNTECLERE & PERTELOTE VS. BIRD-BRAIN SCIENTISTS
Report filed by: Carter Revard, April 1, 2010

A husband and wife who emigrated from Southeast Asia to England, and who (as attested by Geoffrey Chaucer, Esq., quondam Controller of Customs in London) have been living and singing amorous duets in the domicile of a widow, in a village near London, since 1395 A.D., have filed a lawsuit for slander against an international team of scientists led by senior author Richard K. Wilson, PhD, director of Washington University's Genome Center, and Wes Warren, PhD, research professor of genetics at Washington University's Genome Center.

Chaunteclere and Pertelote state that in an article published in the journal *Nature* (vol. 464, 1 April 2010: see APPENDIX, below), Drs. Wilson, Warren, and co-authors, have wrongly represented them as merely clucking and totally without ability to sing, when it has long been known, as Master Chaucer and many ear-witnesses have affirmed, that they are among the finest singers in England. They will offer in evidence one of their most famous duets, *My Lief ys faren in londe*, which they have sung before King Richard and Queen Anne, most recently during a royal entry into and progress through London. They have also sung in America, most recently in Oklahoma, as reported in a review by Signor A. Tommasini, honorary citizen of Pawhuska: "Not since Melchior have we heard a Heldentenor of such power and plangency, and not since Melba a throat with the beauty of Pertelote's."

It is reported that many eminent writers and artists will participate, as *amici curiae*, in the lawsuit. Chaunteclere has mentioned, as one of them, Pieter Breughel the Younger, who will place in evidence his *Adoration of the Magi*, a video of Chaunteclere singing from the stable roof in Bethlehem on the first day of January in Zero A.D. (The sound quality of this demands faithful listening.)

It is not yet clear what sums the complainants will ask in damages, but some of the scientists named in the lawsuit believe it will be settled for a nominal sum and a public apology. However, lawyers with some knowledge of the case have hinted that the scientists may be sentenced to perform brainscans of Pertelote and Chaunteclere at an upcoming recital in Carnegie Hall, during which it is said they will be singing hilarious new rap-inspired songs about tonedeaf scientists. They will insist that they depend on perspiration as well as inspiration, and have come to Carnegie Hall by the classical highroad: Practice, Practice, Practice.

APPENDIX

Tweet: Scientists decode songbird's genome
March 31, 2010. By Caroline Arbanas

The zebra finch, which gets its name from the black-and-white stripes on the male finch's throat, is the first songbird to have its genome decoded. The project was led by scientists at Washington University's Genome Center.

Nearly all animals make sounds instinctively, but baby songbirds learn to sing in virtually the same way human infants learn to speak: by imitating a parent. Now, an international team of scientists led by Washington University School of Medicine in St. Louis, has decoded the genome of a songbird—the Australian zebra finch—to reveal intriguing clues about the genetic basis and evolution of vocal learning.

An analysis of the genome, published April 1 in the journal *Nature*, suggests a large part of the bird's DNA is actively engaged by hearing and singing songs. The simple melodies last only a few seconds but are rooted in tremendous genetic complexity, the scientists report. The new work provides insights to help scientists understand how humans learn language. It also sets the stage for future studies that could help identify the genetic and molecular origins of speech disorders, such as those related to autism, stroke, stuttering and Parkinson's disease, the researchers say.

"Now we can look deep into the genome, not just at the genes involved in vocal learning, but at the complex ways in which they are regulated," says senior author Richard K. Wilson, PhD, director of Washington University's Genome Center. "There are layers and layers of complexity that we're just beginning to see. This information provides clues to how vocal learning occurs at the most basic molecular level in birds and in people."

Among songbirds, singing is almost exclusively a male activity: Males serenade females with love songs to attract a mate. As babies, they learn to sing by listening to their fathers. At first, a young bird "babbles," but with practice learns to closely imitate his father's song. Once the bird has mastered the family song, he will sing it for the rest of his life and pass it on to the next generation.

Aside from humans and songbirds, other animals known to communicate by vocal learning include bats, whales, elephants, hummingbirds and parrots. Because zebra finches learn to sing in a predictable way and many of their genes are conserved in humans, they are an important model for understanding vocal learning in humans.

"The zebra finch genome will be a valuable tool for neuroscientists," says lead author Wes Warren, PhD, research professor of genetics at Washington University's Genome Center. "They can now carry out studies to identify a core set of genes in the zebra finch brain involved in both hearing and producing song and then look to see if any of these genes are disrupted in people with speech disorders."

In their investigation of the zebra finch genome, the scientists demonstrated that the act of singing or hearing a song activates large, complex gene networks in the bird's brain. Past research has shown that hundreds of genes light up in the zebra finch brain as the bird learns a new song. Now, as the investigators looked across the entire genome, they could see hundreds more genes—some 800 in all—significantly engaged by the act of singing.

To the researchers' surprise, many genes activated by bird song do not act like genes in the traditional sense and code for proteins. Instead, DNA from these genes is transcribed into short stretches of non-coding RNA that control the expression of other genes in the zebra finch brain involved in vocal communication. Among the genes suppressed in the moments after a zebra finch hears a new song, two-thirds are non-coding RNAs, the researchers noted.

Non-coding RNAs already are known to play key roles in developmental processes in humans and in animals. They also have been thought to play a role in the evolution of higher organisms.

"Because vocal learning is found in some of the most complex organisms, non-coding RNAs may be a driving force behind this phenomenon," says Warren, who also helped organize the genome sequencing effort.

The zebra finch is only the second bird to have its genome decoded. The first was the chicken, which also was sequenced at Washington University's Genome Center. The two birds split from a common ancestor about 100 million years ago, and their genomes share many characteristics. Both are tight, compact and roughly one-third the size of the human genome: 1 billion units of DNA in the birds versus 2.8 billion in humans.

Interestingly, both birds lack the nervous system gene neuronal protein synapsin 1, a member of a family of synapsins that have been linked to schizophrenia and seizures. This gene has been found in humans and all other animals whose genomes have been sequenced to date—mammals, amphibians and reptiles, including the crocodile, a "sister" to birds in the evolutionary tree. Comparative studies with other animals suggest that the gene was lost eons ago in an ancestor to modern birds, perhaps in dinosaurs capable of flight.

Unlike the chicken, which clucks but does not communicate by vocal learning, the zebra finch retains a great amount of flexibility in the brain to learn bird song.

A comparison of the zebra finch and chicken genomes also reveals some profound differences and suggests several paths through which evolutionary forces may have combined to produce birds capable of vocal learning.

These include the accelerated evolution of ion channel genes in the zebra finch brain, which are known to play important roles in behavior and neurological function; the way genes on the male sex chromosomes are expressed; and the duplications of genes in the zebra finch that produced new variants of neurobiologically important genes.

"We don't have the complete picture yet," Warren says. "Scientists will need to determine when these characteristics arose during avian evolution and what their significance is. This work would not be possible without having the complete zebra finch genome in hand."

Also on the horizon is the sequencing of the parrot genome, which is slated for completion later this year. That project is a collaboration between Washington University's Genome Center and Duke University.

Washington University *Record*, April 1, 2010

THE BODY POLITIC
OR,
EVOLUTION IN JEOPARDY?

I'm waiting for Alex Trebek,
on the TV program JEOPARDY,
to stage another contest between
the IBM program called *Watson* and a few
human *idiots savants*.
The Final Jeopardy Question,
for the category *POLITICAL BIOLOGY*,
would be:

A word for a mechanism used to monitor ion-flow within human cells,

or traffic-flow between East and West Germany,

or between Palestine and Israel,

or between Republicans and Democrats,

or (perhaps?) an ATM.

The correct answer: "What is a **CHECKPOINT**?"

Notes to **The Body Politic**

Researchers in Cell Biology use the metaphor "checkpoints" for places on the metaphoric "ion channels" (i.e., "streams or roads" along which neural "messages" travel) where the "traffic" is figuratively inspected for any "improper or illegal" items. In the human body, when such CHECKPOINTS go wrong (should we think of this as corrupt Customs Inspectors at an international border, or failures of body-scanners at a Security checkpoint in an airport?), the result may be such body-disorders as "cystic fibrosis, epilepsy, migraine, abnormal heart rhythm, type 2 diabetes and a range of other disorders." Biologists are now researching how, at these CHECKPOINTS, damaged cells "can attempt repairs or self-destruct to prevent that damage from leading to cancer."

APPENDIX
Appointment of New Head of Cell Biology etc. Dept. in Med School

Piwnica-Worms' goals for departmental development include prominent roles for two Biomed 21 research centers, the Bridging Research with Imaging, Genomics and High-Throughput (BRIGHT) Institute and the Center for the Investigation of Membrane Excitability Disorders (CIMED). The BRIGHT Institute is making state-of-the-art technology from a variety of fields available for study of the molecular roots of cancer, while CIMED is dedicated to the study of how flaws in cell structures called ion channels can contribute to cystic fibrosis, epilepsy, migraine, abnormal heart rhythm, type 2 diabetes and a range of other disorders.

"Imaging is going to be an important part of our mission," Piwnica-Worms says. "We are looking forward to working with the basic science departments and the Mallinckrodt Institute of Radiology to provide the research community with imaging capabilities that bridge the spectrum of proteins, cells, animals and humans."

Piwnica-Worms' research has helped show how mechanisms known as checkpoints interface with the cell cycle machinery to delay the cell's progress through its life stages. The delays provide cells with important opportunities to inspect their DNA for damage. If damage is detected, cells can attempt repairs or self-destruct to prevent that damage from leading to cancer.

Piwnica-Worms earned a doctorate at Duke University Medical School and did postdoctoral research at the Dana-Farber Cancer Institute. Prior to her appointment at Washington University in 1994, she held appointments at Tufts University School of Medicine, Harvard Medical School and Beth Israel Hospital.

from Washington University *Record*, March 10, 2011

MEADOWS, MOTHS, SLATEBEDS, DICTIONARIES
For Lois and Bill Winchester

On May Day when I walked around our meadow at Buck Creek, some wintered-over lace-grass was there alongside the champagne gold bluestem, above the new ankle-high green, between the blue and pink and gold blossoms just opening, the small milkweeds almost blooming. The lace-grass stems (if that is what those were) are almost white, and there were many small white moths fluttering through and just above the grass and flowers—as I walked, I saw one start up next to my foot, flutter a little way ahead, then dive down into the sparse grass and vanish. Only when I stepped aside right where I saw it disappear, and watched it start up again, did I see how it vanished: it caught onto a white grass-stem, fan-folded its wings completely, and was just another grass-stem until I stooped and looked close. It's a one-dimensional chameleon-trick that seems meant to fool the swallows dipping and swerving after the meadow's insect-feast. Some of the small butterflies, the blues or hairstreaks, have another trick, not by umbrella-folding wings to become grass-stems, but by shutting the bright-colored top-wings up against each other so that only the very dull bottom-sides show, and those among brilliant flowers almost disappear when they perch motionless. Bright topwings open for sex-dances, gray underwings keep them from getting mugged.

And as my friend Bill says, "poignant" is a good word, less rusty than "poniard"—but as Emerson remarked, back when etymologists were just learning how to unfold the feathers of Archæopteryx from the lexical slatebeds, every word is at first a poem, which we notice at age two but forget by age twenty. Even the word "cliché" was not a cliché, but (as Hamlet says of his Mouse-Trap play) "tropical," came forth hot from the Satanic mill as "a stereotype block; a cast or 'dab'; esp. a metal stereotype of a wood-engraving used to print from"—which, in its tropical mutation, became "*b. fig.* A stereotyped expression, a commonplace phrase 1892." Thus saith the *Shorter OED*. And the *Encyclopedia Britannica*, speaking of "printing," dives into the technology of "stereotyping" in lovely detail, as much fun as watching a white moth vanish and magically reappear out of the meadow: here is the word, fluttering up again from its ancient slatebed. What was it Blake wrote: "Truly, my Satan, thou art but a dunce: Every harlot was a virgin once"—and, *Measure for Measure*, clichés were poems once. Like moths fluttering, like swallows flickering.

FROM THE EXTINCT VOLCANO, A BIRD OF PARADISE.

Notes to **Meadows, Moths, Slatebeds, Dictionaries**

The extinct volcano of that last phrase is in New Guinea. It is called Mt. Bosavi, is 8,500 feet high, and since its last eruption 250,000 years ago the crater, some three miles across, has gradually become a terrestrial paradise where hundreds of new species of plants and animals have been evolving, including a giant vegetarian rat, fanged toads, and a Bird of Paradise. It is a fine role model for old poets, or Phoenix Arizona, for that matter.

SONGS OF THE WINE-THROATED HUMMINGBIRD
with thanks to Alexander Skutch's The Life of the Hummingbird

Down in the sapphire ocean
 the Humpback whales are singing,
 maybe about the wonders there,
 how light changes as they descend so that
 their silver day becomes
 a sable night,
or about those whippersnapper bottlenoses blowing
 great shimmering bubbles then piercing like
 spears the silver-quivering
bag of a rising bubble—even as high within
 its green radiance of Guatemalan forest
 a wine-throated
 hummingbird's "sweetly varied outpouring
 continues for the better part
 of a minute"
 —ah, if only
 the whales and dolphins swam
 in that green light and heard
 those tiny singers in their sea of leaves,
 such arias they'd interchange,
La Ci Darem La Mano from a great dark whale,
Un Bel Di from high in the frangipani—and then,
 imagine the duets,
 O Terra Addio at the top
 of a dolphin's range, in the center of
 a rubythroat's fioritura—
 of course
 they sing together only
in human words, never I guess in any
 but English ones in fact—
in these, if anywhere. Can you hear,
 dear reader, how
they sing, you above all who from Africa
 brought banjoes and picked up saxophones
 then sang the blues all out
of slaveship holds to Harlem, you from every

ocean and continent who understand the songs
of police and ambulance sirens, who record the stars
or white noise from the first Big Bang, is it beyond
imagining how the humpback and
the hummingbird might come out
through parted curtains at the Met for a last
encore? What are sounds,
and what are songs, that we can make them,
that we have ears to hear,
that on these tiny waves
of air, of water, even of magnetism, we have made
the smaller ripples that we call Meaning
when sounds are words—or which, rising
like Aphrodite from the foam
of dance and song and love, come through as Music? Deep
in the blue Antarctic seas, high
in the green Guatemalan jungle, here
in these cracked English words,
can you hear them sing,
the hummingbirds, the humpback whales,
a neutron star, a human soul?

HE SHOULD OF DRUNK GOAT'S MILK MAYBE
a pastoral elegy for the Bard of Buggerall, and all our D.T. relations

Good thing we were in a Lincoln Zephyr—Dylan couldn't ride a horse worth a damn, particularly after a pint of white lightning and two hours in the back seat bonking our hottest local poetry lover. I had stopped the car to accommodate the action in both front and back seats, and since our front seat finished first, I climbed out to take a leak and figure out where we were—been a while since I was down this back road from Bartlesville to Pawhuska. The MKT tracks ran alongside us here so I knew we were not far from Okesa, the best place to locate some more moonshine before we went by Nelagoney and maybe stopped in to pay our respects to the Lookout family and go on to Pawhuska for our June dances there. He would not admit that our Osage songs and dances were like an Eisteddfod, but he was happy with a scarlet ribbon-shirt and the blanket our folks gave him when we called him out to the drum on the fourth day.

"This is about where old Elmer McCurdy stopped the Osage Payroll Train," I said to Dylan and our avid poetry lovers. Dylan was sitting up alongside Barbie and she had just lit a cigarette and handed it to him. He was not looking over at the train tracks, he was looking fifty yards ahead on the red clay and gravel road, at a pair of huge luminous green eyes that showed up when I turned on the car-lights, just where the lights went dim.

"Is that a mountain lion?" he asked. The eyes abruptly rose, disappeared six feet above the road, then reappeared hurtling toward our windshield. Dylan screamed, but they flashed past with a sound of wings as he dived down onto Barbie's lap and she broke out laughing.

"Only a whippoorwill," she said.

"Oh, shit," he said. "I thought this was Indian Territory."

"It is," I said. "That's Old Elmer's ghost, he's still mad because the Osage Payroll was not on that midnight train he stopped over there on the tracks, they put it on a later one. All his bunch got was the conductor's watch and a case of good whisky. He rode off on his own with a couple of quarts. Kept him warm in the cold rain with the posse not too far behind him. Rode twenty miles through the hills to my Grandpa Charley's ranch up north, hid in the haybarn loft and finished off the whisky. They tracked him down, sent my father age ten out to the barn, asked Elmer to come down and answer a few questions. He said come and get me, but he was too drunk to shoot straight, their rifleman got him. They dragged him down, took him in a wagon down to Pawhuska and left him in the funeral home. Nobody claimed the body, they embalmed it. Stood him up in a corner for a couple years, then a traveling circus owner lied that he was a cousin and would give pore old Elmer a decent burial. Took the body and made it a sideshow exhibit, famous bankrobber's corpse, toured the country and made a lot of money. Finally sold it in Hollywood to a funhouse, they thought it was just a dummy corpse, painted it with Day-Glo greeny paint and hung it over the Tunnel of Love with screechy sound effects to scare the lovers floating beneath."

"Let's drive out there and see him."

"Nah, they went out of business in World War Two, not scary enough. Took the body down, arm-bone fell out and they had to get a coroner's report. Traced him to the Pawhuska funeral home, shipped him back, gave old Elmer a famous funeral and buried him in Boot Hill down in Guymon. We could go look at his grave but this whippoorwill is probably old Elmer still looking for that Osage Payroll. They always called him a Goatsucker, same name they give Whippoorwills. Story was that when Elmer was hiding out after he blew the door off the wrong bank-safe, there was an old bootlegger that kept nanny-goats back in these hills, and Elmer used to go at night and squirt goat-milk in his mouth to cure a hangover."

"I'll drink to that," Dylan said. He was still drinking to old Elmer a while later when he kicked the bucket in New York City. Last words were, "This is my thirty-ninth straight bourbon. I believe that's a record. Here's to that lonesome whippoorwill Elmer," then fell off his stool so they took him to the hospital and killed him with the wrong medication. Nobody else in that bar knew who he meant, but three of his Welsh friends have told me they hear a bird crying most nights in Laugharne. Not like a seagull they say, not at all.

TERRACE HAIKUS, CHÂTEAU DE LAVIGNY

1.
Brilliant afternoon,
I'm eighty, this June Solstice—
sun does not stand still.

2.
Lavender mead-hall:
dimpled spider, fat and white,
drinks a honeybee.

3.
Fat caterpillar
chomps green leaves, hopes to become
chartreuse luna moth.

4.
Golden orioles
dive into trellis, vanish
as Mont Blanc appears.

5.
Ilsa: Time Goes By—
I'm in Casablanca—meet
me Burkina Faso?

Note: Number 5 haiku seems to be a tweet from a "British" cuckoo who was tracked in migration from England to West Africa. His radio signals disappeared between Casablanca and Burkina Faso, where (the studies show) cuckoos winter before returning to England.

The sundial on the terrace has this couplet engraved on it:

Let others mark the storms and showers,
I only count the sunny hours.

Photo by Bob Bensen

Carter Revard, Osage on his father's side and with Ponca relatives, grew up on the Osage Reservation in Oklahoma, where he graduated from a one-room school in the Buck Creek Valley. In 1952 he was given his Osage name by his grandmother, Mrs. Josephine Jump, earned a B.A. with honors from the University of Tulsa, and won a Rhodes Scholarship to Oxford University (Oklahoma and Merton 1952). In 1959 he took a Yale Ph.D. and from 1956 to 1997 taught English and American Indian Literature at Amherst College, Washington University St. Louis, and as visiting professor at Tulsa University and the University of Oklahoma. His publications include *Ponca War Dancers; An Eagle Nation; Family Matters, Tribal Affairs; How The Songs Come Down;* and most recently, *From The Extinct Volcano, A Bird of Paradise.*